Ancient Peoples and Places

WESSEX

General Editor

DR GLYN DANIEL

Ancient Peoples and Places

WESSEX

BEFORE THE CELTS

J. F. S. Stone

72 PHOTOGRAPHS
17 LINE DRAWINGS
AND 5 MAPS

T&H
London
THAMES AND HUDSON

THIS IS VOLUME NINE IN THE SERIES
Ancient Peoples and Places
GENERAL EDITOR: DR GLYN DANIEL

SECOND IMPRESSION 1963
PRINTED IN GREAT BRITAIN
BY THOMAS FORMAN AND SONS LTD
NOTTINGHAM

CONTENTS

ILLUSTRATIONS

FIGURES

Foreword

SHORTLY BEFORE his sudden and unexpected death in June 1957, J. F. S. Stone had completed the draft text of a book for the *Ancient Peoples and Places* series. As close personal friends of long standing, we had agreed that I should read his first draft and that we would then discuss such modifications or alterations as might be thought necessary. A typescript ready to be sent to me was among his papers at his death, and following our original plan, and with Mrs. Stone's warm approval, I took over the MS. and such illustrations as he had collected for the book to prepare it for the press. Originally conceived as a *Prehistoric Wessex,* the book had evidently developed in the author's mind as a study of somewhat more restricted scope for which the title *Wessex Before the Celts* was more appropriate. The book therefore appears under this title, and my part in its preparation has been limited, so far as the text is concerned, to certain modifications of archæological interpretation and emphasis which in any event would have resulted from our joint revision, and the inevitable tidying-up of a draft not yet in its final version. Essentially, however, the book which now appears represents the volume planned and written by J. F. S. Stone.

STUART PIGGOTT

Author's Preface

THIS BOOK ON PRE-CELTIC WESSEX does not attempt to deal in detail with the archæology of the region which has been covered very adequately by L. V. Grinsell in his recent *Archæology of Wessex*. Its aim instead is to present in small compass a summary of its earlier prehistory, of man's gradual control of his environment in this most vital region of Britain that in later centuries was to witness the birth of English history. But even though a coherent picture of continuity of life and endeavour is slowly emerging as a result of relatively recent excavations and study, it cannot be denied that the task of writing the book has proved a formidable one. The very richness of the region in prehistoric remains has of necessity imposed limitations and has called for rigorous selection from vast quantities of material accumulated by numerous students whose work it has been impossible to acknowledge individually in the text though it has been included as far as practicable in the reasonably full bibliography appended.

Some may feel that clarity has been sacrificed by the inclusion of too much detail. I cannot hope to escape this criticism. Others may justifiably consider many of the statements made to be too dogmatic. Here I can only beg the reader to bear in mind that future work is bound to modify many of the inferences drawn from present inadequate data. We are still only on the threshold of a true appreciation of man's past, and I would therefore wish this short essay to be viewed in the light of an introductory chapter written to stimulate interest in, and further study of, so momentous a region. It is indeed no exaggeration to say that Wessex has acted as a seed- or hotbed for a very long time, receiving the full impact of Continental and foreign stimuli, invasive and otherwise, that have in the sequel shaped in no small measure the course of British history. The emergence and growth of the character of the rural population with their strongly marked conservatism, stubbornness, common sense and love of freedom can be dimly discerned in these early pages, and it is on such characters that much of British history rests.

I have been fortified in the attempt to sketch the rhythmic ebb and flow of early Wessex fortunes by a personal background of some thirty-six years of excavation experience in the region. This, however, might have proved relatively sterile but for the most generous help and encouragement of Professor Stuart Piggott who has not only allowed me to peruse his relevant chapters of the forthcoming monumental *Victoria County History of Wiltshire* but has also accepted the onerous task of reading through and criticizing the manuscript.

J.F.S.S.

CHAPTER I

Savage Wessex

FEW CAN VISIT WESSEX without at some place or another being impressed by the very large tracts of open chalk downland that dominate much of the landscape and which are centred on Salisbury Plain. So large are they that they comprise major parts of Wiltshire, Hampshire and Dorset, counties which, with the addition of the eastern part of Somerset and the chalk escarpment of Berkshire, are usually regarded as falling within the general term of 'Wessex'. *Fig. 1*

The characteristic features of these chalk-lands are undulating stretches of softly-rounded contours intersected by combes and valleys, with steep slopes towards their edges rising sometimes to heights above 900 feet. The thin layer of soil that covers the chalk rock is not likely to have supported more than a sparse covering of vegetation with local patches of scrub or gorse which would tend to thicken in the damper watered valleys. Isolated clumps of trees and small woods no doubt relieved the somewhat monotonous scenery on certain restricted and local areas that still retained their capping of Tertiary clay-with-flints. Thus these chalk areas would prove ideal for primitive agriculturalists and stock-breeders, and could relatively easily have been brought under control with a minimum of effort and with the help of grazing beasts.

But heavily wooded country almost completely surrounded these comparatively open and desirable downs, the varied underlying geological deposits favouring the growth of timber. Nevertheless, access to them was not difficult; in fact, their ready accessibility was later to become the major cause of the gradual rise of this part of Wessex to European eminence during the early Bronze Age of these islands. As will appear in the sequel, the Christchurch Avon through the New Forest gave access to the English Channel and northern France; the Bristol Avon to the Bristol Channel and so to South Wales and Ireland; and the Thames, with its tributary the Kennet, to the North Sea and northern Europe. Coupled with these three major river routes were certain overland ways equally suitable for relatively unimpeded movement; one wide chalk belt ran through Cranborne Chase to the Dorset Downs and so to Weymouth; another across the Hampshire Downs to the South Downs and the Sussex coast; and yet a third along the Icknield Way to East Anglia. On the west, a thinning of the woodland near Frome, which has come to be known as the Frome Gap, gave access to the open limestone hills of Mendip. Whilst the northern part of Wiltshire could gain direct access, along the Jurassic Way, to Lincolnshire and Yorkshire, this route does not seem to have been much used until later times.

Fig. 1

Salisbury Plain in particular thus occupied a most advantageous position on a natural trans-peninsular route capable of linking the rich metalliferous lands of the west of Britain and especially of Ireland with the Continent, and of receiving stimuli from a number of widely separated quarters. It would indeed have been surprising, with such potential wealth at its doors, if this region had not been at some early stage of its history exploited to the full.

Wessex, and especially the chalk areas, did indeed attract settlement, and an endeavour will be made in these pages to sketch in broad outline man's interactions with his environment in this immensely important region, from the Mesolithic period to the dawn of the Iron Age. As Professor Piggott has so pertinently observed, 'Wessex has attracted the archæologist and presented him with some of the most complex problems of his study for a good three hundred years and will continue to do so. If we ever succeed in understanding the prehistory of Wiltshire in detail, we shall have gone a long way towards understanding that of Britain.'

However, long before the potentialities of the chalk-lands for settlement and agricultural purposes had been realized, man had roamed southern England in search of food. Excluding evidence of seasonal Palæolithic occupation which does not concern us here, the first glimpse we get of human activity is of groups of savages concerned solely with the quest for food; hunting, trapping and fishing as a precarious means of livelihood. It would seem that the coasts, rivers and woodland alone attracted them for their quarry and it is, therefore, not surprising that the chalk downlands were to a certain extent avoided. By the time of the wet Atlantic climatic phase of the Mesolithic period, when the greater part of northern Europe was still heavily forested, two main groups of such hunters and food-gatherers have been recognized, traditionally separate but later having to a certain extent coalesced through insular isolation. Their cultures are defined largely by the type of flint implements they used: a very small light blade or flake industry with battered points and microburins (microliths), and a heavy core-axe industry where sharpening of the edges was carried out by transverse blows (*tranchet* axes and later, locally, 'Thames picks'). The earlier microlithic industries (related to the French Sauveterrian) and their products are scattered fairly uniformly over the greater part of Britain, and these form part of a generalized epi-palæolithic flint industry centred in France. On the other hand, the Forest Cultures of northern Europe of Maglemosean tradition (a name derived from the settlement-site of Maglemose in Denmark) had developed their characteristic *tranchet* axes, transverse arrow-heads and bone tools recognizable as harpoons, and perforated antler hammers.

These Forest Cultures, in Britain classified as the Lower Halstow forest culture, occur for the most part on our eastern coasts, and by way of the Thames settlement was made over the sandy areas of Surrey, Sussex and Hampshire, in time intermingling with the older microlithic tradition. In Wessex evidence of occupation is found along the Thames and Kennet to Thatcham, Hackpen Hill and Windmill Hill on the Marlborough Downs, and thence to Chippenham, Bath and Wraxall, all on the Bristol Avon and suggesting that this major riverine route, to become of such importance later, had already become a recognized trackway to the West. Further west still, microlithic industries are known along the southern Welsh coast; and at Nab Head in western Pembrokeshire they included *tranchet* axes comparable with one from Penwith in Cornwall. The Mendips, the North Somerset coast around Porlock, and inland at Middlezoy near Bridgwater, have also yielded chipping sites including *tranchet* axes.

Even the clay-with-flints capping of the South Downs between Butser and Winchester was not shunned, though so far in this region only Oakhanger near Selborne on the Hampshire greensand has yielded extensive chipping floors. The high concentration of chipping sites and *tranchet* axes on the Isle of Wight and on the banks of the Solent are considered by W. F. Rankine to be connected with the ancient, but now submerged Solent River system with its Frome, Stour and Lower Avon tributaries. Riverine penetration to Salisbury Plain is attested by finds along the Nadder, Wylye, Upper Avon and Bourne valleys; and of the Lower Avon to Armsley near Fordingbridge and possibly Downton. A very important chipping site has been discovered at Iwerne Minster on the River Stour.

Fig. 1

Although no dwellings similar to the shallow scooped wind-shelters excavated at Farnham in Surrey have yet been found in Wessex, there is no reason to doubt the probability of their existence. Pits associated with microliths have been recorded from Beaulieu, and have recently been found by P. A. Rahtz at Downton, though these need further examination; and the extensive chipping floors at Oakhanger and Iwerne Minster are at least suggestive of their possible presence. Very much more work needs to be done on the identification and the distribution of these Mesolithic hunters in Wessex.

The opening-up of trackways, mainly riverine, by these hunters and their acquired knowledge of the coastline was later to become of supreme importance, and we must include also their tentative recognition of the properties of certain stones other than flint. In their seasonal movements to Devon and Cornwall they seem to have been attracted by certain siltstone pebbles which they collected and brought back with them to their Farnham and other camping grounds. So too the Greensand Chert of the Blackdown Hills in Somerset and the Haldons in Devon appears to have been utilized and dispersed as implements mainly to the West. Portland Chert from Dorset, on the other hand, though less extensively used, was nevertheless carried to the Isle of Wight and to the Farnham settlement.

Certain quartzite 'maceheads' with hour-glass perforations must also have been included in their equipment. One, made of fine-grained sarsen, was found in 1883 in peat 20 feet below the estuarine mud of the Ocean Dock at Southampton, whilst another came from the Mesolithic site at Thatcham. Many such 'maceheads' or small club-heads have been found in Britain in less satisfactory associations and these are mainly concentrated in East Anglia and in the Western Weald though a few are known from Wessex. W. F. Rankine has suggested that some may have been derived from the Bunter Pebble Beds and seem carefully selected for symmetry and suitability for perforation.

The hunting population can at no time have been large; and of their spiritual aspirations we have no inkling in southern Britain. No graves have yet come to light; and the only objects found, other than their hunting equipment, have been a number of small perforated shale discs as if for a necklace, and an object, possibly a phallus or a degenerate figurine, from Nab Head near St. Bride's in Pembrokeshire, all of which may have been derived from contemporary Neolithic settlers in the district and are suggestive of cultural and chronological overlap.

CHAPTER II

First Farmers

THUS FOR THE GREATER PART of his existence man as savage had been entirely dependent upon his skill in hunting or fishing, with his food supply eked out no doubt with roots and berries. Constant movement and a total absence of husbandry would have limited population increase and inhibited any incentive or desire for an alternative mode of life.

However, during the eighth and seventh millenniums B.C., observations by a few appreciative minds in the Near East that seeds could be collected, grown and stored for future use, that animals could be domesticated, selected and bred for special purposes, and, subsequently, that vessels could be artificially made of fired clay for the storage of food and drink, caused an unparalleled revolution in human domestic economy. Freed at last from the uncertainties of the chase and of their effects on the well-being of his immediate family, man could begin to learn to co-operate with his fellows, to specialize in certain pursuits, and to find time to speculate on his existence. Present indications are that the Natufians of Palestine were the first to appreciate the potentialities of primitive cereals, and that at very early levels at Jericho primitive stone-built villages were developing even at the pre-pottery stage about 7000 B.C. The resulting Neolithic agricultural economy, with nature at last coming under partial control, very gradually spread from these Near Eastern centres over the steppes from South Russia to the Baltic, up the Danube to Central Europe, and along the Mediterranean coasts to Iberia and southern France, where by the middle of the third millennium B.C. agricultural communities were still scattered over the countryside with high concentrations around the Swiss lakes and down the Rhine.

About 2000 B.C., with at least one thousand years of literate urbanized civilization behind it, Egypt had already entered upon her Middle Empire, and the XIth Dynasty ushered in a period of great prosperity in art, sculpture, architecture and literature. Crete, too, had entered her Middle Minoan phase with a stone-built palace at Knossos. Both of these urbanized centres needed ever-increasing supplies of raw materials and by one means or another sent out expeditions to trade with less civilized societies, to open up sources of supply, chiefly metalliferous, and to exploit them when found. New waves of more advanced technological culture were thus set in motion, which were shortly to overtake the last ripples of the earlier agricultural revolution that by this time were just reaching remote Britain and the North.

It is now more or less generally accepted that the first seeds of this slowly advancing Neolithic agricultural economy were implanted in southern Britain somewhere before 2000 B.C., the immigrants who brought this New Stone Age culture from France being ultimately of long-headed 'Mediterranean' stock. As yet, however, they were ignorant of, and uninfluenced by, a desire for metals such as gold, copper and tin, at that time so much sought after by the ancient civilizations of the East: a quest soon to revolutionize western European technology, and thence that of Ireland and the British Isles.

The native Mesolithic food-gatherers, no doubt sporadically at first, must have witnessed and viewed with suspicion the canoe-loads of farmers, their families and livestock coasting along our southern shores and seeking likely landing places. Opposition can have been but slight in view of the low population density and of the totally different economies of the two societies. In any event we know that landings and consolidation proved successful from Devon to Sussex, and that this immigration was almost certainly dictated by the necessity for new grazing grounds and less impoverished land. Burning down scrub and light woodland can for a few years maintain fertility of the soil for small-scale garden hoe-culture, but gradual movement to fresh sites is essential. So, also, fresh pastures have to be found for cattle when the vegetation grows sparse.

The relatively unoccupied and open chalk downlands naturally attracted attention and were in fact deliberately chosen for their easily available pasturage. On them we have considerable evidence of the colonists' activities. The primary area of settlement was thought to be on Windmill Hill, near Avebury on the Marlborough Downs which, owing possibly to the priority of modern excavation, has given its name to the earliest Neolithic culture found in these islands (in the past termed Neolithic A). But recent trial excavations in a similar enclosure at Robin Hood's Ball near Stonehenge have shown that it also belongs to the same early culture, seemingly uncontaminated by later occupation, and may represent an earlier phase of the gradual spread of the immigrants to the North.

At any rate, in the deepest levels of the ditched enclosure crowning Windmill Hill the characteristic forms of round-
Plates 1–4 bottomed, bag-shaped, leathery, mainly unornamented pottery found there are now recognized as belonging to the great Western Neolithic series of ceramics, the nearest comparable material being that of the Early Cortaillod Culture found round the shores of Lake Neuchâtel and elsewhere in Switzerland. Generalized forms of this ware occur in many parts of France, but regional variants, and our lack of knowledge of comparable sites along the northern coast-line, make it extremely difficult to identify any specific region of embarkation for the makers of the particular forms found at Windmill Hill and in comparable sites on the Sussex Downs. Similar wares occur in enclosures at Maiden Castle in Dorset and at Hembury Fort in Devon, but these often possess 'trumpet lugs' which are unknown at Windmill Hill and in the Cortaillod Culture. Hence it seems most probable that the immigrants who

built these two western ditched enclosures must have come from farther west in Brittany, where similar lugs are found; whilst the immigrants to the Sussex coast seem more closely connected with north-eastern France and Belgium. The answer to the problem will no doubt be clearer when we know more of the archæology of northern France, but we should not underrate the conscious absorption of new ideas and equipment gleaned from the native Mesolithic population on both sides of the Channel with whom the peasants must occasionally have come into contact. As Professor Toynbee has emphasized, regional variants in equipment and the development of new institutions are inherent in the special stimulus imparted to immigrants by transmarine colonization; cleavage from old traditions and absorption of new ideas not infrequently accompany such migrations.

These ditched enclosures, also known as causewayed camps, are one of the chief manifestations of the Windmill Hill Culture in southern England though exact parallels are not encountered on the Continent. It is true that somewhat similar earthworks of the interrupted-ditch type form part of the Michelsberg Culture in Germany, but this culture is of later date and cannot be considered as ancestral to that of Windmill Hill. But there may be ancestral elements shared in common by the cultures of Michelsberg and that of Windmill Hill, with origins in the north European plain; in Britain these traditions may have mingled with those of Cortaillod or French derivation. On Combe Hill near Eastbourne a causewayed camp is known to have been dug and occupied by a group of people whose pottery may have North European affiliations. *Fig. 1*

Of the thirteen examples of such earthwork enclosures known, six lie in Wessex and all crown well-defined chalk hill-tops commanding extensive views. Others, no doubt, still await discovery. They consist of single or multiple, more or less concentric, lines of discontinuous ditches with undug causeways separating them, and these ditches appear to have been originally dug as quarries to form embanked enclosures within. Owing to long-continued weathering and silting-up they are not easy to see on the ground except at Knap Hill near Alton Priors and at Windmill Hill itself, where the excavations by A. Keiller in 1924-29 have until recently been preserved in approximately their excavated state. Here we have triple lines of ditches, the outer as much as 8 feet deep, and enclosing an area about 1200 by 1000 feet. On the other hand, Maiden Castle and Robin Hood's Ball have two only, whereas those on Hambledon Hill, Whitesheet Hill and Knap Hill possess single circles apiece. All have been tested by excavation, though only Maiden Castle and Windmill Hill extensively.

The contents of the ditches at these last two sites, which are flat-bottomed with vertical sides, proved illuminating and enable us to form a reasonably clear picture of life at the time and of succeeding, but otherwise unrelated, Stone Age peoples who settled in the same areas soon after the enclosures had fallen into disuse and had become derelict. Although never intended for permanent occupation, the refuse in the lowest primary levels shows that seasonal squatting by small groups of people had caused much of the accumulation as in corresponding sites on the Sussex Downs. Besides numerous fragments of the characteristic pottery vessels already noted, temporary hearths were encountered, as well as quantities of animal bones, and stone and bone tools. It is the presence of these very numerous bones of domesticated animals that gives us a possible key to an understanding of the basic economy of the culture, that of stock-breeding. There is no evidence that these earthworks with their interrupted ditches were constructed for defensive purposes, or for permanent settlement, but they are explicable as cattle-kraals for easy sorting and herding.

The bones, often split for marrow, of oxen, sheep, goats and pigs are represented; but it is the number of slaughtered cattle, frequently killed by pole-axing, and especially of calves, that gives us the clue. The absence of cultivated roots and winter feeding-stuffs necessitated an annual round-up of the herds and the slaughter of excess stock; the latter practice continued until a couple of centuries ago in these islands. One can picture the intense seasonal activity centred in and around these enclosures; with dogs barking, cattle being driven in for selection of future breeding-stock and slaughtering of the unwanted, the dismemberment of the carcasses for food, and the feasting. The women no doubt prepared the skins for new leather clothing for the winter and for making into ropes, since no evidence exists of any form of spinning or weaving. Flax was grown, but probably for its nutritious oily seeds rather than for its fibres. Leather-working almost certainly formed an essential part of every woman's occupation; the presence of numerous flint scrapers for preparing the hides, and of antler-combs for removing the coarse hair from the skins, and still used for a somewhat similar purpose by the Esquimaux, are evidence not only of skill in leather-craft but also of another instance of a normal Mesolithic hunter-fisher art having been taken over by the immigrants to cope with the rigours of a British winter.

The species of domesticated animals first introduced into these islands are of considerable interest. They must have been brought over the Channel in canoes, presumably as young livestock only in the first instance, as a full-grown cow or bull would hardly have commended itself as a voyage companion. The cattle appear to have been of the small, long-horned type related to the primitive *Bos primigenius,* but this calls for more research. The sheep seem to have been the same as the 'Turbary Sheep' of the Swiss Neolithic (*Ovis familiaris palustris* Rut.), and the pig a small form agreeing also with the Swiss Neolithic breed (*Sus scrofa palustris* Rut.). The dog, of which complete specimens have been found at both Maiden Castle and Windmill Hill, was of a large fox-terrier type and identical with the

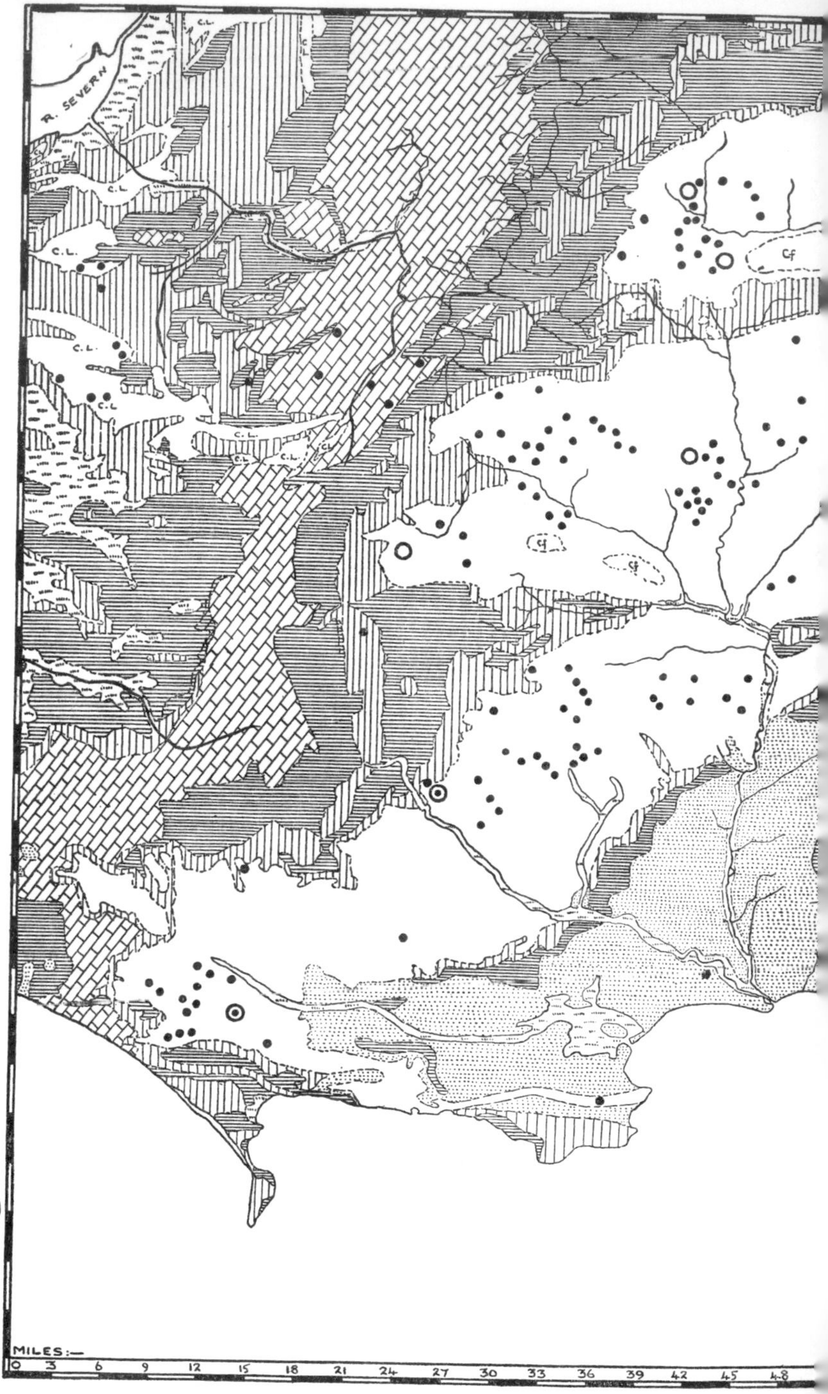

Fig. 1 The natural background of Wessex, and the distribution of long barrows (dots) and causewayed camps (circles)

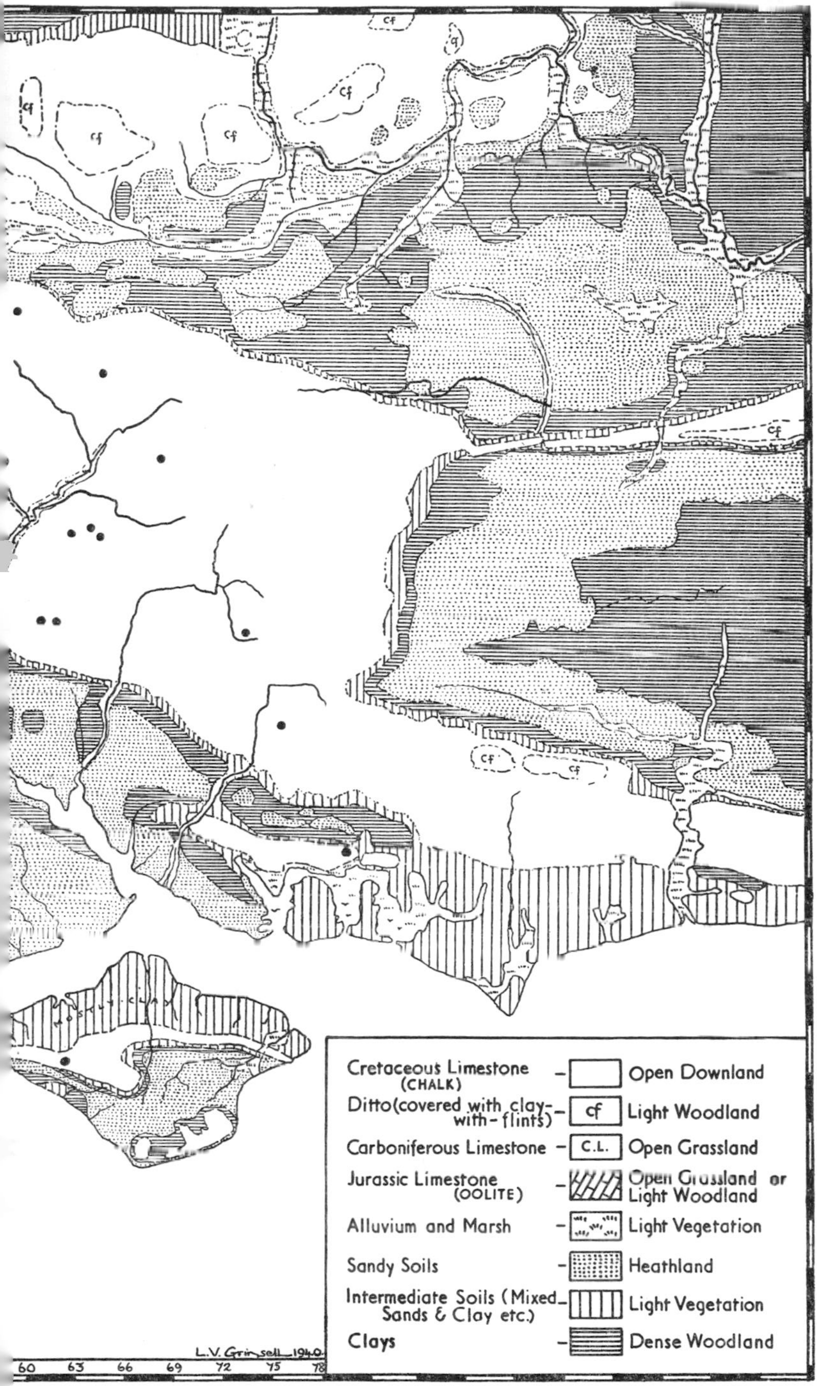
Cretaceous Limestone (CHALK) – Open Downland
Ditto (covered with clay-with-flints) – cf – Light Woodland
Carboniferous Limestone – C.L. – Open Grassland
Jurassic Limestone (OOLITE) – Open Grassland or Light Woodland
Alluvium and Marsh – Light Vegetation
Sandy Soils – Heathland
Intermediate Soils (Mixed Sands & Clay etc.) – Light Vegetation
Clays – Dense Woodland
L.V. Grinsell 1940
60 63 66 69 72 75 78

Swiss *Canis familiaris palustris* Rut. No evidence exists for the domestication of the horse in the Windmill Hill Culture.

Our evidence for corn-growing and for the introduction of cereals comes from the presence of a few grain rubbers of sandstone and from an examination of grain impressions on pottery; Windmill Hill has produced so far the greatest number of identifiable impressions—one hundred and twenty-seven in all—from sites of the culture. Wheat appears to have been the principal product, amounting to more than nine-tenths of the cereal total, with Emmer (*Triticum dicoccum*) the commonest, Einkorn (*T. monococcum*) a very modest second, and probably a contaminant of the former. Barley amounted to only ten per cent of the cereals, naked barley being commoner than the hulled form. Two large flax seed impressions have suggested comparison with similar seeds grown in the Swiss Neolithic and indicate its cultivation, probably for food; apple-pip impressions suggest that crab-apples were included in the diet.

No signs of permanent occupation have been found in these enclosures, and no large rectangular timber structures, similar to those at Köln-Lindenthal and elsewhere on the Rhine, have been located except in the case of the fragmentary remains of a possible one on the edge of the Easton Down flint mines near Salisbury, which we shall note later.

More significant, however, are proved contacts with the West. On the Mendips, there was a temporary cave shelter at Chelm's Combe, and the post-holes of some form of structure at Chew Park are clearly linked with the timber-built oval and rectangular houses at Clegyr Boia near St. David's, Pembrokeshire almost in the shadow of the Prescelly Mountains, whose significance for Stonehenge will be apparent later. Even then these mountains must have loomed large as a landmark or potent magic beacon to those venturesome enough to brave a sea passage, since similar settlement sites and house types are known in Devon and Cornwall and even at Lough Gur, Co.

Limerick, which indicate that the southern shores of the Irish Sea were by no means unknown or unfrequented by Neolithic colonists and voyagers at the time.

Timber for the construction of canoes, stockades, buildings and other purposes was at all times obtainable provided that felling equipment was easily and continuously made available; and we must not forget the obvious necessity of forest and scrub clearance. Raw material in the form of flint lay ready to hand in seams in the chalk, but it is not now clear that the specialized industry of flint-mining for the purpose of satisfying the demand for flint axes was initiated by the Windmill Hill people and as the industry was certainly greatly expanded by succeeding Stone Age cultures, we may defer further comment for the moment. At all events, flint alone was used for the manufacture of axes at Windmill Hill itself and in the causewayed camps of Sussex, whereas at Maiden Castle and Hembury Fort in Devon polished stone axes of igneous rocks also make their appearance, again suggestive of west, rather than north-east, French influence. But the wide use of leaf-shaped arrow-heads on all contemporary British sites and their absence in Brittany implies derivation from eastern France and Belgium where they were freely used, as was also the practice of flint-mining. It is clear, as we have already noted, that our local primary Neolithic phase resulted from the combination of a number of cultural traits. The Windmill Hill Culture may well embody the elements derived, on the one hand from the 'Western' Neolithic cultures represented in France and Switzerland, and on the other from the early 'Northern' cultures of the North European plain. Nor can we ignore the potential contributions of the older hunting cultures of Mesolithic origin.

CHAPTER III

Family Tombs

THE SPIRITUAL BELIEFS and magico-religious practices of the Windmill Hill people, though somewhat meagre and contradictory, are of considerable interest. The disposal of the dead is a case in point. Here we have to balance the seemingly callous and casual way in which a few bodies were interred amongst the accumulating refuse of the ditches of the causewayed camps, against the very careful preservation of many of their dead and subsequent burial in specially constructed and laboriously built tombs. Cannibalism also seems to have entered into their primitive beliefs, though this is difficult to prove. Signs of fertility cults, natural to pastoral stock-breeding societies, are not infrequently encountered.

Besides the burial of a dwarf in the primary silting of the outer ditch of Windmill Hill, a number of human bones were found there scattered throughout the occupational debris. Cranial fragments predominated in many of the camps, especially at Whitehawk in Sussex where a number were found with animal bones, pottery and burnt flints close to a hearth and charred by fire. One cannot escape the conclusion that some form of head-hunting must have been practised and formed part of the Western Neolithic Culture since similar cranial fragments, including cranial amulets, have also been recorded from France and Switzerland; and later we shall note the disproportionate number of skulls to lower jaws in the West Kennet long barrow. Fragmentary skulls and broken human bones have even been found in the British flint mines; at Grime's Graves in Norfolk a human femur had been used as a pick to lever out the chalk.

Probably the best authenticated example of apparent cannibalism comes from Maiden Castle. Here, under the eastern end of an enormously long and aberrant mound 1790 feet in length and 65 feet wide, overlying the ditches of the causewayed camp but generally contemporary with it, Sir Mortimer Wheeler in 1937 found three burials; two of children and another of a young man 'who had been systematically dismembered immediately after death. The bones bore many axe marks, and the whole body had been cut up as by a butcher for the stew-pot. The skull had been hacked into pieces as though for the extraction of the brain . . . all the parts were present. Save where they had been hacked off, the limbs were still in articulation, as were the divided halves of the spine. The impression given at the time of discovery . . . was that the body had been cooked and eaten.' Subsequent anatomical examination confirmed that a number of unsuccessful attempts had been made to extract the brain until finally this was accomplished through the base of the skull.

Such, then, are the scanty indications of practices that have suggested head-hunting and cannibalism, though clearly it would be unwise to be too dogmatic until we know more. So let us turn to the more normal methods of burial of the Windmill Hill Culture.

In contrast to the inconspicuous seasonal cattle-kraals, long barrows form the most numerous and prominent landmarks of the downland scenery. Compared with Sussex, which possesses some twelve examples only, Wessex can boast at least one hundred and sixty scattered from the Dorset Downs to the north of Wiltshire with a few outliers on the Mendips introduced no doubt from this primary area of settlement through the Frome Gap. A solitary long barrow at Holdenhurst, near Christchurch, which O. G. S. Crawford long ago pointed out must have been the port for the Dorset and Wiltshire Downs, and one on the Purbeck Hills, serve to emphasize the remarkable concentration on the chalk downlands. A few small isolated groups in Lincolnshire and Yorkshire are the only others known in Britain. *Fig. 1*

Yet ten of these barrows are sited within a radius of 2 miles of Stonehenge, suggesting that even at this early date the region had acquired a measure of sanctity. Now, excavations in 1953 round the undressed monolith at Stonehenge, known as the Heel Stone, proved that this had been erected in Beaker or even pre-Beaker times; three years later a sherd probably of Windmill Hill ware was found at the base of a disturbed area close to the same stone and could be taken as suggesting that this monolith antedated the first phase of Stonehenge, until recently known as Stonehenge I. The implications of this most remarkable fact are not only that the site may already have been selected for some ritual purpose by the Windmill Hill colonists with their causewayed camp 2½ miles away, but that even at this early date they may have seen fit to undertake the laborious task of transporting a huge natural block of sarsen from the Marlborough Downs, a feat to be repeated much later on a more grandiose scale but one which was well within their grasp from the experience they had gained in the building of the West Kennet chambered long barrow near Avebury, which we shall shortly describe.

Fig. 10

In Wessex we have to draw a sharp distinction between the chambered and unchambered varieties of long barrow, which, in the absence of excavation, are not always easy to distinguish from external features alone. The former, in general a small minority, are confined to the Marlborough Downs especially round Avebury, while the latter cover a very large part of the remainder of the chalk downlands to the south, the two groups being separated by the dry greensand Vale of Pewsey, a by no means insurmountable barrier, yet one that accounts for many differences between the two regions.

Let us first consider the more numerous unchambered group which consists of long mounds with flanking ditches that sometimes continue round one end, and from which the material of the mound was obtained. Some may be nearly 500 feet in length, others less than 100 feet, whilst most are higher and broader at one end than the other. Often they are sited on conspicuous crests, less often on lower, flatter ground. Though normally isolated, some are intimately associated with earthen structures of the Cursus type, and others, especially round Stonehenge, with later round-barrow groups suggesting that the sanctity of these areas continued into Bronze Age times, as in the Normanton, Lake and Winterbourne Stoke groups. *Fig. 9*

Our knowledge of their internal features is derived mainly from South Wiltshire where thirty-seven were excavated early last century by Colt Hoare and later by Thurnam, in a somewhat rough-and-ready manner. Nevertheless, their results, analysed by Thurnam, are of value and can be interpreted in the light of more recent work especially by Pitt-Rivers's total excavation of Wor Barrow, and later in barrows at Thickthorn, Holdenhurst and elsewhere. But further scientific work is needed in this field, and more comparative material.

A distinctive internal feature appears to be a thick layer of decayed turf or humus piled along the axis at ground level or, as at West Kennet, a similarly placed ridge or spine of stone boulders. In Bowl's Barrow near Heytesbury a similar ridge of stone boulders included the very remarkable block of Pembrokeshire 'preselite' weighing upwards of 5 cwt and now in the Salisbury Museum, petrologically identical with many of the 'bluestones' at Stonehenge and implying that it was locally available for incorporation in the barrow during its construction. Pits in the barrow floors, interpreted as fulfilling some ritual purpose, have been found in a number of them, whilst in one at Warminster a standing stone 5 feet high had been erected.

Communal burial of anything from two to twenty-four individuals on the floor and under the higher end appears to have been the normal practice, though at Winterbourne Stoke one inhumation alone was found in a mound 240 feet long.

Very frequently the bodies appear to have been mixed up together, a large proportion of the bones being disarticulated. Colt Hoare noted that many were 'strangely huddled' or 'lying in a confused and irregular manner', whilst in Bowl's Barrow Thurnam recorded a heap of disarticulated bones representing some twenty-four individuals, some of which were without flesh when buried.

This mode of collective burial of articulated and disarticulated bones together, of people of all ages and sexes, can best be explained on the assumption that the burial rites involved a two-stage process; the gradual accumulation of the dead of a tribe or family in temporary mortuary houses, and their subsequent final burial with elaborate funeral ritual under a long barrow. The completion of the barrow can be considered as the final rite, the denial for ever of further access to the dead. What determined this final act we do not know; seemingly it could take place with feasting after a single death, or not until a whole generation at least had died. In any event, the recent recognition of these mortuary houses or enclosures has added appreciably to our knowledge of contemporary ritual. The houses themselves appear to have been long rectangular wooden structures, or ditched and banked enclosures, which were sometimes buried under the mound itself as at Wor Barrow on Cranborne Chase. Here, Pitt-Rivers found an enclosure of small posts set in a bedding trench and enclosing an area 90 feet by 35 feet with an entrance to the south-east.

At other times the ritual seems to have involved the partial cremation of the bones or temporary contact with purificatory fires. This has been noted in five Wiltshire barrows, the heaps of bones having been placed on platforms of flints. Grave-goods were rarely placed with the dead, fragments of broken pottery, presumably scattered during some ritual act, are found on occasion, and these belong consistently to the Windmill Hill Culture. Nevertheless, it still remains a moot point whether communal burial in long barrows formed part of the originally introduced culture. The origin of the unchambered barrows remains obscure. There is no reason to suppose that they were derived from the Severn-Cotswold chambered cairns, and few have as yet been recognized in northern France except in the Morbihan region of Brittany. Here, especially at Manio near Carnac, long, low mounds cover rectangular-shaped enclosures within which are numerous burials in stone cists with pottery of the undecorated Western Neolithic type and comparable with Windmill Hill ware. These and other features inclined Professor Piggott at one time to the view that these mounds must in some way be connected with the unchambered long barrows of England. But he has recently pointed to similarly comparable barrows in the early Neolithic cultures of the North European plain. Plates 1–4

However, while the colonists were infiltrating along our southern shores, related groups were moving up the Atlantic coasts and, coming from the Loire estuary, they settled in the Severn-Cotswold region. With them they brought the elements of a Megalithic religion, a cult involving the use of massive stones for the construction of collective chambered tombs, for the burial of their dead. These so-called 'long barrows of the Cotswolds' are very well documented and have received most careful attention in recent years. They are built mainly of local oolite or other Jurassic rocks and in form approach the trapezoid or rectangle with the wider end incurved to form a forecourt, behind the centre of which is the burial chamber in the typologically early forms, or a 'false portal' in the later. The edges of the cairns are usually delimited by dry stone walling or peristaliths, whilst the chambers themselves are built of orthostats, with dry-walling between, to carry capstones or a corbelled roof. As in unchambered barrows, burial was collective, bones of as many as forty-eight persons having been found in one cairn at Tinkinswood. Whilst grave-goods Plate 5 are scarce, the pottery is again consistently Western Neolithic and related to that of Windmill Hill.

Plates 1–4

The main concentration of these chambered cairns lies outside Wessex to the north of Tetbury, but a fine example of a southern outlier exists at Stoney Littleton, near Wellow, into which access is still possible. In spite of extensive restoration in the nineteenth century this tomb gives a very good impression of the type. The gallery is here nearly 50 feet long with three pairs of transeptal chambers, the roof being a corbelled barrel-vault.

Before their final closure and elaborate ritual blocking, the interiors of these tombs must have been readily accessible. Successive burials took place in them and, when full, the bones of previous occupants were pushed aside. Thus in one small chamber ($4\frac{3}{4}$ by $3\frac{3}{4}$ by $2\frac{1}{2}$ feet) at Lanhill near Chippenham, nine individuals of a single family, and ranging from one to seventy years in age, had been packed away at the rear, whilst an articulated skeleton, the last burial, occupied the front half of the chamber.

At a very early period this new cult involving the use of collective chambered tombs impinged on, and coalesced with, the practice of burial in unchambered long barrows to form the chambered variety around Avebury, on the headwaters of the river Kennet, where suitably large blocks of sarsen sandstone lay promiscuously on the surface of the downs. Here we have a compact group of some nine surviving or recorded barrows built of chalk rubble from the flanking ditches, as in the south, but embodying stone-built chambers in the Cotswold style.

The West Kennet barrow is one of the largest and most famous examples. Although partly explored by Thurnam in 1859, it was not carefully excavated by modern standards until 1955-56, when it was found that four chambers fortunately still remained completely intact and undisturbed. This excavation by Professor Piggott and R. J. C. Atkinson, has in fact proved to be one of the most interesting and informative of recent years; and the Ministry of Works, in whose hands the guardianship rests, has restored most admirably the impressive gallery and chambers for inspection by visitors. Plates 6–8

The mound itself is 340 feet long, built of chalk quarried from the two parallel flanking ditches which are separated from it by a wide 'berm', and possesses a spine of rounded sarsen boulders running along its length. From the centre of a façade of massive upright stones at the east end, a gallery nearly 8 feet high runs below the capstones inwards for some 40 feet and is terminated by the end chamber excavated by Thurnam. On either side of the gallery four separate chambers, forming double transepts, were found to be filled almost to the capstone roofing with humanly inserted deposits, the stratigraphical relationships of which confirmed similar but naturally occurring cultural deposits observed elsewhere, especially at Windmill Hill nearby. Plate 6 Plate 7

The floor of each chamber was covered with a jumbled mass of human bones, often with skulls pushed into the back recess; and potsherds of early Windmill Hill types, including a bowl of developed Abingdon style with shell grit, accompanied them. Thirty disarticulated skeletons were found in the four chambers and, surprisingly, more lower jaws were present than skulls, suggesting that some of the latter had been removed, possibly for ritual purposes. Over these lay successive layers of occupational refuse, apparently placed as a ritual act and derived from outside the tomb. These had apparently been inserted intentionally, as each was separated by layers of comparatively clean sterile chalk rubble which could not have silted in naturally in the quantities observed. Pottery of the later Secondary Neolithic Cultures of both Peterborough and Rinyo-Clacton types, including Bell-Beaker sherds, some with cord-zoned ornament, were fairly plentifully strewn in these Plate 8 *Fig. 5* Plate 11

later layers with charcoal, animal bones, beads, bone pins and
Plate 14
spatulæ; whilst an almost complete Bell-Beaker lay on the topmost layer under the corbelled roof of the north-west chamber. In the absence of natural agencies, these distinct and separate layers are only explicable on the assumption that the tomb retained a degree of sanctity for some years and that later peoples occupying the district saw fit to perpetuate the memory of the dead by scattering token remains of their feasts in the chambers. In any event, the important feature is the relationship of the early Windmill Hill pottery with a tomb of the Severn-Cotswold type, a relationship that is not yet susceptible of exact solution.

At a late date in its history the final rite involved the closure of the entrance to the tomb. This consisted in the erection of two further massive stones in the forecourt, continuing the line of the passage, and the emplacement transversely across and in front of them of colossal blocks weighing upwards of 20 tons apiece, to form a sort of false entrance. Owing to the shallowness of the holes into which the latter were placed, and the thrust of the mound behind, some fell outwards at an early date. However, the experience gained by the builders in this complex operation, and in the emplacement of massive capstones on vertical uprights, may well have contributed to the tradition of skill involved in the setting up of the stones of Avebury itself, later to culminate in the creation of Stonehenge—to which, as we have seen, the Heel Stone may already have been taken. But such operations needed much timber for packing and leverage, and it is of interest to observe on some of the West Kennet orthostats the highly polished markings and grooves where flint or stone axes had been sharpened and reground.

But the effort involved in terms of man-power was not confined solely to the construction of these laboriously built tombs for collective burial. The cult of the dead occasionally demanded very much greater effort, the burden of digging immensely elongated enclosures with which certain long barrows are intimately associated. The Stonehenge 'Cursus', discovered and so called in 1723 by Stukeley, who likened it to a racecourse and so gave it the name now used for this type of structure, lies about half a mile to the north of Stonehenge. This banked and ditched enclosure, nearly 1¾ miles long, 110 yards wide and enclosing 70 acres, lies on undulating ground and is terminated at its eastern end by a long barrow. A small trial excavation in 1947 showed that the ditch had been dug by gangs of workers with deer's-antler picks to form a continuous inner bank, causeways having been left here and there, confirming indications on aerial photographs. The remains of a flint chipping floor were also found on the bottom. *Fig. 9*

This enclosure pales into insignificance, however, when compared with that of the Dorset Cursus which runs from Bokerly Down to Thickthorn Down, a distance of fully 6 miles, and encloses 220 acres. Here, too, the ditches and banks are separated by about 100 yards and run parallel, though much of it is now ploughed out. The labour and tribal organization involved must have been immense; it has been calculated that a volume of some 6½ million cubic feet was extracted for the banks and this may be compared with the 3½ million dug from the Avebury ditch. One striking feature of this cursus is that it is bipartite; at some stage it must have been decided to double its length from Bottlebush Down, where parts of the earthwork can still be seen. Four long barrows are included in it: one at each end, that on Bokerly Down being the longest on record (490 feet); one at right angles on the crest of Gussage Down; and a fourth included in one of the banks. This intimate association of long barrows with cursus earthworks, known also in Oxfordshire, is strong presumptive evidence of contemporaneity. Their purpose we can only guess at; possibly some form of processional way, a conception later to be translated into avenues of stones. But we can be certain that they were used for religious ceremonial rather than for domestic or agricultural purposes.

We can also be sure that the same impelling religious urge occasionally called for more personal objects. Chalk figurines, rather crudely carved and possibly representing the Mother or Earth Goddess, have been found at Windmill Hill and Maiden Castle, though they are rare in the Western Neolithic Culture. Carved chalk phalli, probably connected with fertility cults, are also rare but have been recorded from Windmill Hill and from the Thickthorn long barrow. Small chalk 'cups' and pottery 'spoons' or 'ladles' are not infrequently found in both this and the immediately succeeding cultures; it has been suggested that these also may belong to the same class of ritualistic objects as the phallic carvings.

Chapter IV

Flint and Stone

THE OLD DEFINITION of man as a toolmaker is an apt one, for by his tools we can distinguish him from his fellows and gauge his reactions with his environment. In her own words, Professor D. A. E. Garrod has wisely said, 'Man's tools are the instruments of his response to the world in which he lives, but they are much more—they are the weapons of his conquest of that world . . . this is the true drama of prehistory, the clue to its interpretation.'

As the name implies, Western Neolithic man's response to his forest environment was not continued acquiescence in its presence but the conscious introduction of ground and polished stone axes for its control, of types superior to the *tranchet* axes of the Forest Cultures and capable of more effective use. But these axes needed raw materials from which to make them, and in quantities that could satisfy the ever-increasing demand. Flint had been used from time immemorial for the chipping of tools, the special characters of which serve to distinguish one culture from another, though it is not yet possible to distinguish the source of origin of each type of flint with any degree of precision. It occurs fairly abundantly in various regions weathered out on the surface and sometimes, as at Little Somborne in Hampshire, it is obtainable from natural outcrops. Some years ago the remains of a surface workshop was found here, extending over two acres, which turned out 'Thames picks', a type of implement of Mesolithic ancestry not infrequently found on the chalk downs, and contemporary but unconnected with the Western Neolithic Culture.

Plates 10, 12, 13

But such surface flint is of poor quality and flakes badly; the best is obtainable only from seams lying deep in the upper chalk. It is almost certainly to the credit of the Neolithic colonists of North and West Europe, and not to the Forest Cultures, that the properties of these deep flint seams were recognized and exploited, even though traditionally in most of Europe the normal axe was of igneous rock. In their settlement of the chalk regions of Belgium, northern France and southern England, the only raw material immediately available was flint; and it is in these areas that we find flint-mining developed practically for the sole production of axes. Nevertheless, the bone tools used in the mining process, many of the axe forms produced, and certain naturalistic carvings of deer on flint crust as at Grime's Graves in Norfolk, all imply that the colonists were not averse—as we have already seen—to absorbing certain useful Mesolithic traits and benefiting from their acquired knowledge. Further, the very existence of these new mining activities and the specialization entailed clearly shows that at last it had become possible to divert surplus foodstuffs, at least temporarily and seasonally, to skilled workers other than those engaged exclusively on farming and intermittent barrow-building.

No fewer than nine mining sites were known on the Sussex Downs before the discovery in 1929 of the first mines in Wessex on Easton Down 7 miles north-east of Salisbury, to be followed three years later by another large group of 100 shafts or so at Martin's Clump in Hampshire 2 miles to the north-east and on the same ridge of downland. The Easton Down mines have been the more extensively examined; they cover some 40 acres (mainly of unploughed downland), and on the surface appear as hollows surrounded by low banks almost touching each other; the filled-in shafts of the mines lie below.

The process of mining consisted in digging vertical shafts down to a seam of suitable flint nodules by means of deer's-antler picks used as wedges rather than as picks in the modern sense, all the tines but for the brow tine having been removed from either shed antlers or those obtained from hunted and

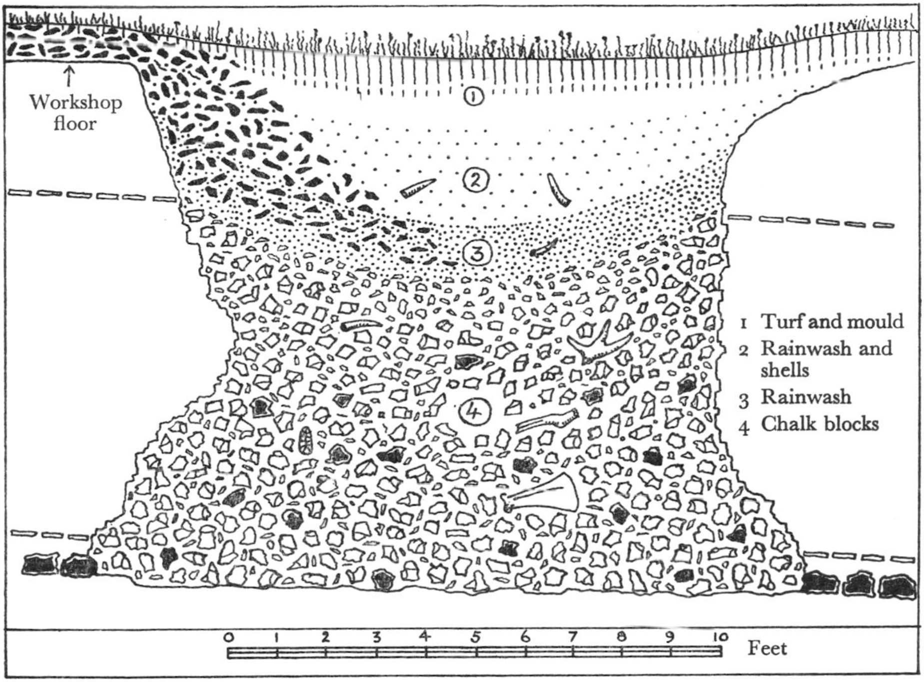

Fig. 2 Section of the filling of a flint-mine shaft on Easton Down, Wilts

slaughtered beasts. To judge by the numbers used and discarded, deer must have been very numerous. The crowns from such antlers were not infrequently used as rakes, and for shovels the shoulder blades of large wild oxen *(Bos primigenius)*. Having reached the seam from 8 to 12 feet below ground level, the base of the pit was enlarged by undercutting to bell-shaped form at both Easton Down and Martin's Clump, to obtain the maximum yield of flint without driving galleries in all directions as was commonly done in the Sussex mines and at Grime's Graves. On the surface and on well defined workshop floors, the extracted flint was then fabricated into axes; the preliminary removal of the cortex and rough shaping would be carried out

Fig. 2; Plate 9

in one area and then passed to another contiguous area for final and more delicate finishing. The last act of grinding and polishing seems very rarely if ever to have formed part of the process; this seems to have been left to the individual taste and requirements of the purchaser, though one such finished product was found in Floor 7 at Easton Down.

From the unweathered chalk walls of the shafts, often still bearing the imprints of the antler picks, and of the chalk blocks filling them, it is clear that the shafts were soon filled in to make room for the next pit. Pottery is not unnaturally rarely found in these industrial workings, though scraps of Windmill Hill ware were found in the rainwash silting at the top of one of them and in the nearby dwelling of a miner. Over this silting lay the workshop floor in which was found the polished axe just mentioned, and a heap of forty-five grey, red and yellow Eocene pebbles—possibly collected by miner's children for a primitive game of marbles!

The mining area is surrounded by settlement sites at Easton Down, the temporary or seasonal dwelling-quarters of the miners. Though initiated by Windmill Hill people, it is evident from the types of pottery recovered that the mines continued to be worked by a number of succeeding cultures including those using Peterborough and Beaker wares; in one instance a typical round-bottomed Windmill Hill pot had been decorated in the Peterborough style thus proving direct overlap of the two cultures.

A fall of a ton or so of chalk from the wall of a shaft during re-excavation rather forcibly suggested insecurity, and that the absence of galleries might here be accounted for on the grounds of safety. But in this the present writer was mistaken. The recent discovery of another small group of flint mines at Durrington, near Amesbury, which had proved relatively abortive in flint, showed that at times it was possible to cut galleries at the flint face only 4 feet below the surface. An outcrop of flint had here been exploited by the open-cast method, and higher up the hill the vein had been followed by sinking shafts and pecking out galleries in the normal manner. This group was discovered during pipe-laying operations; no doubt many others exist though now obliterated by later cultivation.

The primary layers at Windmill Hill have yielded axes of flint only; it was not until the later occupation of the same site by the Secondary Neolithic cultures we shall discuss in the next chapter that axes made from rocks foreign to the district first make their appearance. They have been found, however, in the earliest corresponding levels at Maiden Castle and Hembury Fort, again emphasizing the west French connexions of these camps.

Such axes of rocks other than flint are exceedingly numerous and form a feature of most museum collections; but it was not until the early 1920s that their potential value as trade indicators was appreciated, largely through the pioneer petrological work of H. H. Thomas on the source of the Stonehenge 'bluestones', and by the late Alexander Keiller's recognition of the wider potentialities of the method. As a direct result of this work a committee was formed in 1936 by the South-Western Group of Museums and Art Galleries to study their petrology and distribution in Wessex and in the adjoining counties of Gloucestershire, Devon and Cornwall, with special reference to their probable sources of origin. So productive and illuminating did the work become that the Council for British Archæology in 1945 raised what was virtually a regional monopoly on to a national basis with the direct result that Great Britain has now been regionalized for the purposes of this study and its development.

It has in fact proved to be a most fruitful line of research. Over a thousand specimens have been sliced and examined by the South-Western Committee, and it has been found possible to place well over four hundred of these into twenty-four

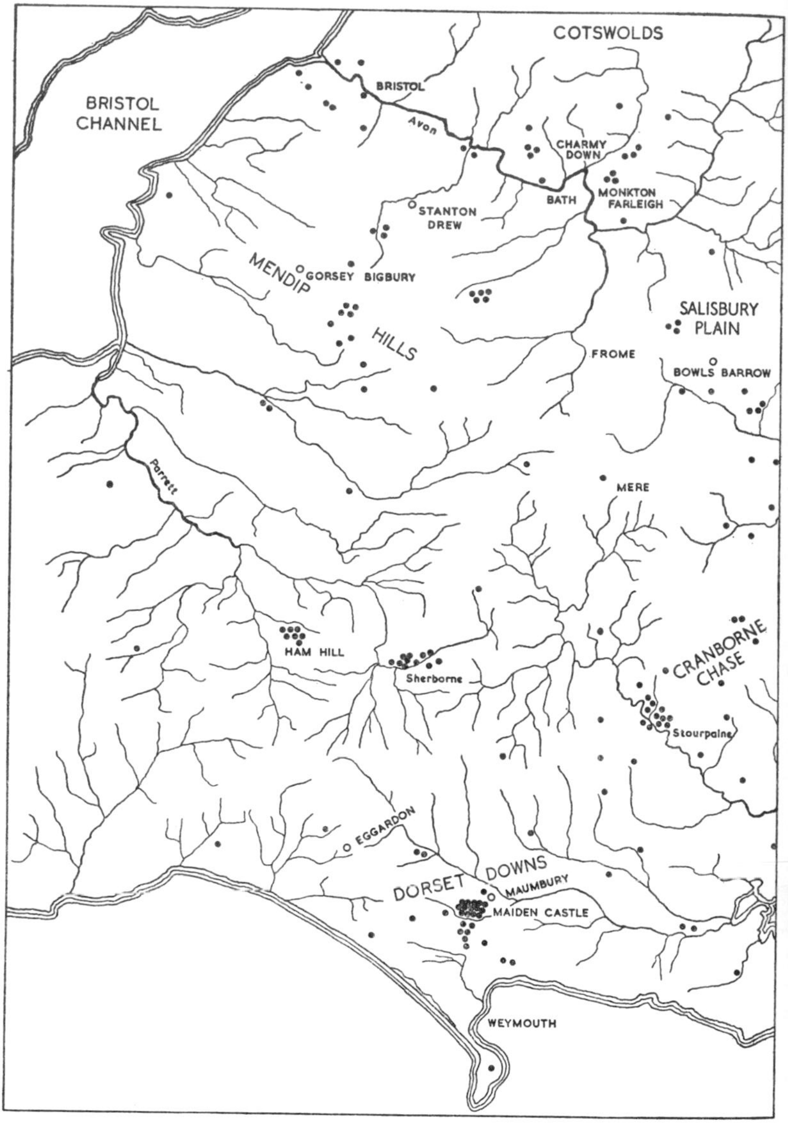

Fig. 3 Distribution of axes of stones geologically foreign to Wessex

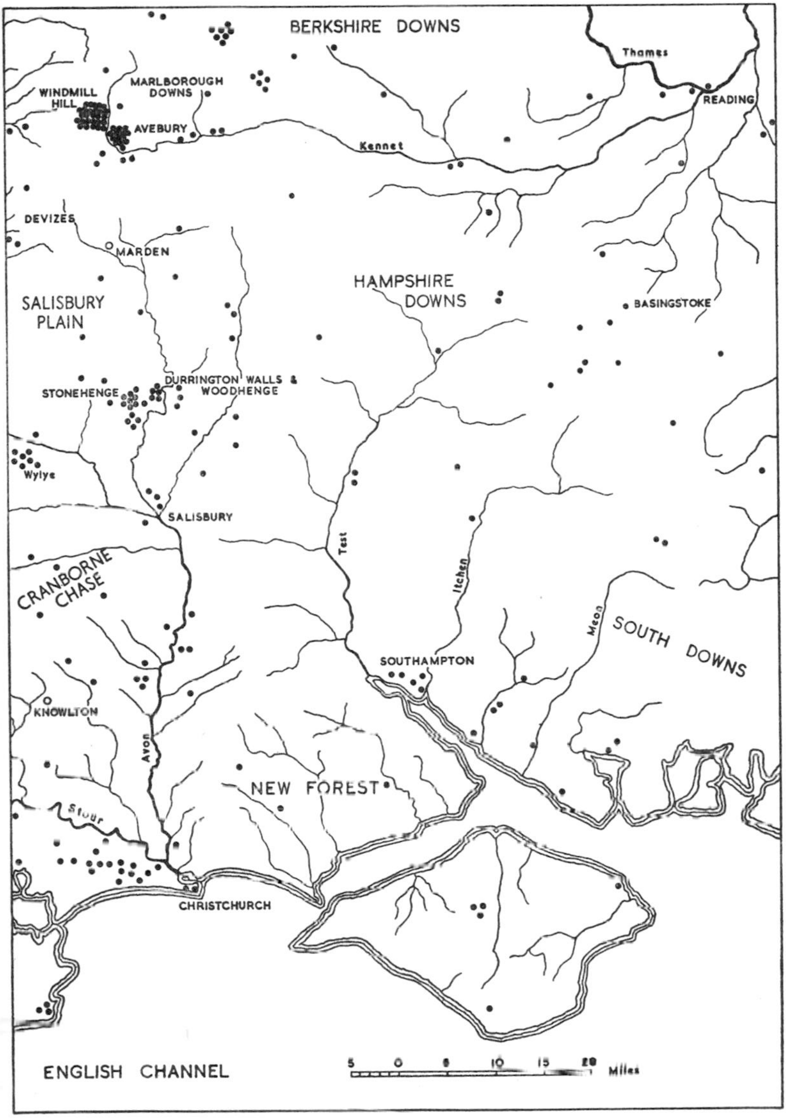
BERKSHIRE DOWNS
Thames
READING
WINDMILL HILL
MARLBOROUGH DOWNS
AVEBURY
Kennet
DEVIZES
MARDEN
SALISBURY PLAIN
HAMPSHIRE DOWNS
BASINGSTOKE
STONEHENGE
DURRINGTON WALLS & WOODHENGE
Wylye
SALISBURY
CRANBORNE CHASE
Test
Itchen
Meon
SOUTH DOWNS
SOUTHAMPTON
KNOWLTON
Avon
NEW FOREST
Stour
CHRISTCHURCH
ENGLISH CHANNEL
5 0 5 10 15 20 Miles

petrological groups which in many instances have been traced to their sources of origin—sometimes well-known factory sites, at other times to outcrops of identical rock. These igneous outcrops and factory sites lie geologically outside Wessex and occur mainly along our western coasts from Brittany to Cornwall and up the Irish Sea to the Lake District and Northern Ireland. Distributional studies of their products, specimens of all of which are to be found in Wessex, thus provide a valuable
Fig. 3 guide to the trade routes over which they were carried and to the cultural contexts in which they are found. Mere cursory examination of the distribution map of all foreign stone axes, irrespective of origin and known to have been found in Wessex, indicates that the main routes of penetration from the primary coastal trade routes were riverine, as would be expected in densely forested country, and follows precisely the same pattern as those of Mesolithic finds. In particular, we should note the concentration of find spots along the rivers Stour and Christchurch Avon, the Kennet tributary of the Thames, and especially along the Bristol Avon, the trunk road as it were to the west.

Trade and movement were indeed widespread and involved even cross-Channel voyages. Certain axes from Jersey, Southampton, Bournemouth and Tewkesbury (Group VIIA) have recently been proved by P.-R. Giot to have emanated from Brittany, whilst it is possible that the ten ceremonial axes
Plate 10 of jade or jadeite in Wessex came from that country also; more work is now being done on these.

On the other hand, Cornwall seems to have been the main source of supply of certain greenstone axes. Small numbers have been proved petrologically to have come from outcrops at St. Ives, from Trenow near Marazion (Group III), Kenidjack Castle near Cape Cornwall (Group XVII), Camborne (Group XVI) and Balstone Down near Callington (Group IV), though the actual factory sites have not yet been located.

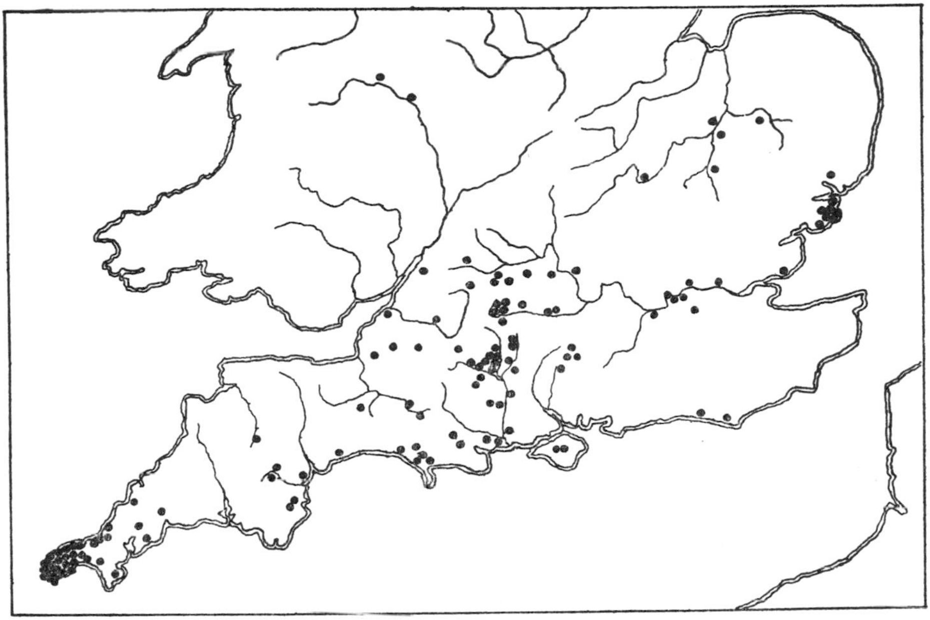

Fig. 4 Distribution of axes of Group 1 in southern England

Two Marazion specimens have been found in Stonehenge and as far afield as Bridlington in Yorkshire. Of far greater importance, however, was a factory turning out the products of Group I, the largest group so far examined and comprising one hundred and six specimens. Their distribution is shown in Fig. 4 from which it will be seen that we are here dealing with a major industrial Cornish activity which found an immediate market in Wessex. Although exact identification has not yet proved possible, there is not much doubt that the factory must have existed in the Mount's Bay region between Penzance and Mousehole where very similar outcrops occur, but probably now submerged below sea-level. This area is known to have subsided (as at Er Lannic in Brittany and around Jersey), and

Fig. 4

the identification of an axe from Salisbury and of a large battle-axe from Okehampton, Devon, as having very probably originated from the Gear Rock, now on the 5-fathom line and about half a mile out in the bay off Penzance, lends colour to the supposition.

This Group I factory, wherever it was, turned out a great variety of products, more so in fact than any other known site or group, and this may well mean that it continued to be worked for some years. Specimens have been found in the secondary occupation layers at Windmill Hill, at Stonehenge, Woodhenge and in another similar ceremonial earthwork at Dorchester in Oxfordshire, and in a few round barrows of the early Wessex Culture, which implies that the factory may have been in the hands of Secondary Neolithic producers.

But Wessex was also importing the products of factories very much farther afield; such long-range connexions may be indicative of a class of trader who found lengthy journeys worth while. Axes from such factory sites as that at Graig Lwyd in Caernarvonshire, from the screes of the Pike of Stickle in Langdale, and even from Tievebulliagh Hill in Co. Antrim are all well represented, and especially so in the Avebury district. These were not necessarily traded overland through the Midland Gap as were most probably Graig Lwyd axes; the high concentration of most types at Bournemouth, and scattered finds round the coasts of Dorset, Devon and Cornwall are strongly in favour of a degree of coastal traffic. At least six have come from the Whin Sill of the Teesdale area; these are mostly of Early Bronze Age (Wessex Culture) battle-axe form, one of which is of great interest as it came from a
Plate 13 round barrow at Upton Lovel in Wiltshire and was directly associated with mullers of both Groups I and IIIA and other early transitional Bronze Age objects.

We have seen already that both Mesolithic hunters and Western Neolithic colonists settled in Pembrokeshire, and we have seen too that this county is dominated by the Prescelly Mountains which have readily accessible outcrops of distinctive volcanic rocks scattered along their crest. The most distinctive of these is spotted dolerite or 'preselite', which outcrops at Carn Meini and Cerrig Marchogion and which contains well-marked white or pinkish felspathic spots of all sizes from that of a pea to that of a walnut. Something about its character must have been sufficiently impressive and significant to warrant the laborious transport to Wiltshire of some eighty large blocks weighing anything up to 4 tons apiece, one or more blocks of which were incorporated in the spine of Bowl's Barrow. More will be said later about these 'bluestones' when we come to consider Stonehenge itself, but what is now clear is that these blocks did not come from a region renowned for megalithic monuments or stone circles. It did, however, produce ground stone axes and—of even more significance, as will appear later—battle-axes of 'preselite'; a large specimen of the latter, weighing 5 lb. 2 oz., was found at Fifield Bavant, and other axes along the south coast from Sidmouth to Bournemouth. Plate 12

Apropos dating the industry, the only axes that occur in the Western Neolithic levels of Maiden Castle and Hembury Fort belong to Groups IIA and IVA, both almost certainly from Cornwall. All other groups examined have been found in Late Neolithic contexts and must have been exploited by Secondary Neolithic people; the products are also more developed and varied, and include perforated axe-hammers, mace-heads and battle-axes.

But before leaving the subject of axes, we must not omit to mention that originally they also possessed a ritual or votive significance, of the content of which cult we now have no inkling. In the Minoan world there was the well-known Cult of the Double Axe, and as a symbol possibly of a deity, the concept of the symbolic axe was common in Europe. In

Brittany, large numbers of magnificent axes made from rare and beautiful rocks were ceremonially deposited as grave-furniture in such Megalithic tombs as those of Mané-er-Hroëk, Mont Saint-Michel and Tumiac, or at the base of standing stones. And not content with burying the actual objects themselves, representations were sometimes carved on the structural stones of the tombs. In Wessex, we have little evidence of the cult except for the otherwise relatively useless but beautiful
Plate 10 imported axes of jade or jadeite, and of others made from softish sandstone or even of chalk as are two from Woodhenge. However, the concept was present and, as we shall see, later found positive expression in carvings of bronze axes on the stones of Stonehenge.

CHAPTER V

Consolidation

IN THE LAST three chapters we have considered the Primary Neolithic colonists and the indelible marks they left behind them on the Wessex landscape. Estimates of the length of their sojourn have been very varied, the most extreme being that of W. A. Sturge, President of the Prehistoric Society of East Anglia in 1909, who confidently stated and considered that he had proved 'on irrefragable evidence' that the Neolithic period had lasted well over 200,000 years—a grossly inaccurate estimate that we now know to be out by a factor of about 1000 and a measure of the distance we have travelled in understanding the chronology of prehistoric Europe since that date. Five to ten generations of men, or 100-200 years, would perhaps be nearer the mark as an estimate of time before these Neolithic peoples had inextricably mingled with the native population or had moved northwards in search of new pastures.

Estimates of vital statistics, in the absence of full information, could be equally inaccurate, and we do not propose to embark on them. However, if we take an average of ten individuals per long barrow, we have tangible evidence of some sixteen hundred burials spread over this much shorter period. This does not represent a very high population density for so scattered a community engaged as we have seen in stock-raising, cereal-growing, digging causewayed enclosures and constructing immense long barrows and colossal cursus earthworks. It is obvious that much man-power remains unaccounted for. Either burial in long barrows was accorded only to the heads of tribes and their families, which is the more probable explanation, or the native population was dragooned and exploited for such navvy tasks as digging earthworks and sinking shafts for flint. The normal estimate of a hunting population as one per square mile would undoubtedly apply to the period before the introduction of farming, and with a total area of 7290 square miles Wessex could no doubt have supported this number of individuals. But there can equally be no doubt that numbers must have greatly increased as a result of the impact of this newly introduced farming economy.

We have, therefore, now to deal with the reverse process; the results of this impact on the native population during and after the recession of the full force of the innovation. The stimulus did indeed call forth responses, varied in character, but all attributable nevertheless to this primary causative impulse. New and distinct 'cultures' suddenly make their appearance, characterized mainly by new pottery forms, and all closely linked by common usage of flint and bone tools of very distinctive but developed Mesolithic types. To these resurgent cultures, some of which were ultimately affiliated to those of what Gjessing has called the Circumpolar Stone Age of the northern hemisphere from Norway to North America, the name of Secondary Neolithic has been given; secondary in the sense that they were derived from the Primary Neolithic Culture by an admixture of peoples who still retained many of their essential Mesolithic characters and traditions.

Wessex was the common meeting ground of these diverse elements and in Wessex we witness their full interplay not only in the early stages of contact but in the later phases of amalgamation, with the subsequent impact of the new Bell-Beaker and Single-Grave invaders from the Continent. Here we need not enter into the minutiæ of their complex interrelationships. It will be sufficient to distinguish three main components which, in spite of regional variants, have been termed the Peterborough (formerly Neolithic B), the Rinyo-Clacton or Grooved Ware, and the Dorchester Cultures, after type-sites where their remains were first recognized. All three contributed their quota to the ensuing vigorous Bronze Age, but none are easy to define in terms of man owing to the remarkable paucity of human remains. All have been found to be consistently later in date than Western Neolithic deposits and fall therefore within the Late Neolithic phase, though some slight overlap is perceptible in Wessex itself. True Windmill Hill ware is now recognized as covering the Early and Middle phases which are both stratigraphically earlier at Windmill Hill and in the West Kennet chambered long barrow than in the overlying Peterborough and Rinyo-Clacton occupation layers.

PETERBOROUGH CULTURE

In origin it is possible to distinguish two main strains in the Peterborough ware as developed in Britain; a combination in fact of the pit-comb ware of Scandinavia—a product of the huge province embraced in the Circumpolar Stone Age cultures—and of the cord-ornamented funnel-beakers characteristic of the great area stretching from South Russia to the Baltic. Both resulted from the impact of Neolithic peasantry on the northern Forest Cultures and both strains seem to have merged after crossing the North Sea to produce forms not characteristic in detail of either province. These folk-movements, for such they must have been, took place largely on our south-eastern shores, the main movement being up the Thames valley to Wessex and the headwaters of the Kennet, and from thence to the Cotswolds.

Pottery of the Mortlake bowl style, developed locally by these people through contact with the later phases of the Windmill Hill Culture in East Anglia and up the Thames, takes the form of thick, coarse, round-based pots with thickened rims and profuse ornament over the greater part of the vessels. This ornament usually consists of twisted or whipped cord impressions, though impressions of the articular ends of bird bones and finger-nail rustication are not infrequent.

If one infers these people to have been in the main of hunting stock, their skill in obtaining supplies of deer's antlers must have been of value in the flint-mining industry where on Easton Down we find their pottery, including a hybrid lugged vessel of Windmill Hill form decorated with whipped cord ornament, amongst the temporary dwellings of Beaker date. We have little knowledge of any permanent settlement. In three small pits surrounded by stake holes at Winterbourne Dauntsey and interpreted as dwellings, Peterborough sherds have been found with a typical flint-mine axe from the nearby mines. In these pits were the bones of oxen, pigs and sheep, which shows that by now they had assimilated the value of domesticated animals; but the remains of myriads of slugs amongst their food refuse presents a picture of unsavoury squalor. Evidence of their presence is also found in the deserted ditches of Windmill Hill, along the course of the West Kennet avenue, and as far south as Cranborne Chase, in Maiden Castle and in the ditches of the Holdenhurst long barrow. Polished stone axes of igneous rocks from the West usually accompany their remains, strongly suggesting that they were the purveyors of such commodities.

Little is known of their burial practices. We have noted their ritual deposits of domestic refuse in the West Kennet long barrow. With this refuse was found a contemporary cremation of two individuals. However, we appear to have a more elaborate burial in a barrow on Handley Down. The fragments of an inhumation were here found under a low barrow surrounded by a very irregular ditch having a wide causeway. Peterborough sherds occurred in the body of the mound and in the ditch silting.

RINYO-CLACTON CULTURE

The second component of the Secondary Neolithic cultures, the Rinyo-Clacton or Grooved Ware Culture, is almost as ill-defined in the south of Britain. Nothing comparable with the Orcadian stone-built houses at Skara Brae and Rinyo with their beds, dressers and other domestic amenities has survived. The culture, which is concentrated in the two widely separated regions of the Orkneys and the south of England with practically

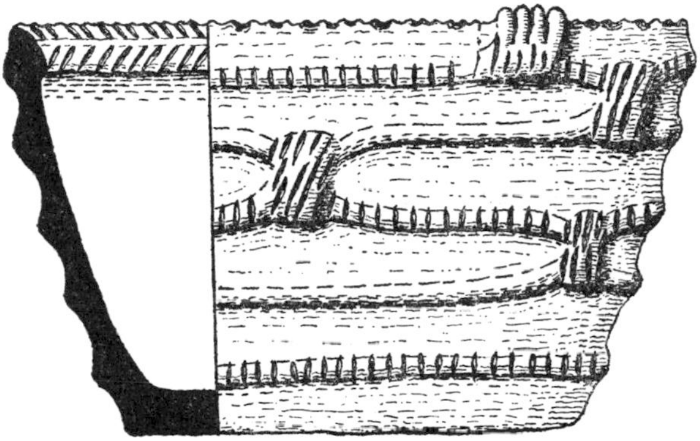

Fig. 5 Cup of Rinyo-Clacton ware from Woodlands, near Woodhenge, Wilts. 2¼ in. high

no intermediate links, was first recognized by its characteristic pottery at Woodhenge and was later seen to be closely affiliated to similar wares from the submerged Essex coast at Clacton-on-Sea near which seven Group I Cornish axes have been found. Pit-comb and cord ornament are here absent, but once again two strains can be distinguished in the pottery, the bases of both of which are flat-bottomed. One strain is decorated by shallow grooving, channelling or incision, including sometimes dotted triangles or lozenges (*pointillé* ornament); the other by a freer use of plastic ornament. The former may be derived *Fig. 5;* Plate 11 from Late Neolithic styles in north-western France and Iberia, whilst the latter is more generalized and with its pinched-up rusticated decoration may well have come from anywhere along the European coast of the English Channel.

It seems probable that the makers of this type of pottery first settled between Weymouth and Christchurch, thence spreading northwards through Wessex; their implements were the flint and stone ones characteristic of Secondary Neolithic culture. One of their most interesting settlement sites lies in the Amesbury district on both banks of the river Avon. Some pits at Ratfyn have yielded Rinyo-Clacton sherds, transverse or *petit tranchet* derivative arrow-heads and bones of ox and pig; and—of unusual interest—the shoulder-blade of a brown bear (*Ursus arctos*).

At Woodlands, within 300 yards of Woodhenge, four pits have been excavated which can only be described as ritual in character. These had been carefully dug and contained a surprising assortment of articles mixed with wood ash and charcoal. They appeared to have been filled by tipping into them baskets of food refuse and of almost unused tools amongst which were a Graig Lwyd axe, a flint axe, a number of *petit tranchet* arrow-heads, flint saws or serrated flakes, scrapers, a flint knife and fabricator, a hammerstone and naturally formed flint balls, and bone pins or awls. The bones found showed that ox, sheep, and pig were eaten, as well as roedeer and fox. Bones of a dog were also found. Fishing activities resulted in numerous jaws of chub. Shells of scallop, common mussel and oyster show that even then these were considered delicacies and that contact with the sea was maintained. The associated
Fig. 5 pottery was also of particular interest; small highly decorated flat-based cups that may well have been the prototypes from which sprang the pygmy cups of the ensuing Bronze Age.

Woodhenge itself produced much plastically ornamented pottery under the bank and in its ditch, with Beaker sherds at higher levels; but Windmill Hill ware was also present, suggesting cultural overlap. Allied ware has also been found under and above the edges of the banks of the contiguous earthwork known as Durrington Walls, along the southern edge of which was a long straight line of 58 post-holes with offsets suggestive of part of a building and associated with similar occupational refuse including an unusually high proportion of pig bones. A few sherds of grooved ware in the primary silting of the ditch at Stonehenge have helped to date the first phase of that monument, as does also the presence of Group I axes here and at Woodhenge nearby. Between these two famous monuments and also to the south of Stonehenge, the surface of the ground still remains a prolific hunting ground for flint implements of Secondary Neolithic date, including *tranchet* axes, *petit tranchet* derivative arrow-heads and other recognized types. The culture is also represented, along with Peterborough pottery, in the secondary occupation layers at Windmill Hill, in the West Kennet long barrow, and in the settlement area along the West Kennet avenue where pits and hearths have yielded similar material with axes from both Graig Lwyd and Great Langdale.

Plate 11

DORCHESTER CULTURE

The third component in Wessex has been termed the Dorchester Culture, named after a number of sites examined from 1946 onwards at Dorchester-on-Thames near Oxford. This 'culture' has been tentatively defined by Professor Piggott to embrace certain features not wholly covered by the other two cultures, though he very clearly recognized that future work might drastically modify its status or even discard it as a distinct and separate entity. It is, indeed, doubtful whether it can be considered to exist in its own right. The future may well show that its manifestations are but imperfectly understood facets of the two Secondary Neolithic cultures we have just considered, the full content of which has not yet been assessed.

The tenuous characters that distinguish this culture appear to be somewhat negative. For instance, no settlement sites are known, and no distinctive pottery can be claimed as an index; Peterborough, Rinyo-Clacton and late Windmill Hill ware normally accompany some of its manifestations. However, on the positive side we have, firstly, communal cremation burials in flat cemeteries often accompanied by rings of holes or pits of a ritual nature never intended to hold stone or timber uprights; these may or may not be surrounded by an enclosure of the ceremonial 'henge' type to be discussed later. Secondly, certain inhumation burials under round barrows or cairns in which single-graves have replaced the collective burial practice of the long barrows.

The recognition and implications of these cremation cemeteries and circles of ritual pits at Dorchester-on-Thames have thrown considerable light on the first phase of Stonehenge which comprises the bank and ditch, Aubrey Holes and cremation cemetery. Although consideration of the latter must be deferred for the moment, it is well to remember that both Rinyo-Clacton ware, typical Rinyo-Clacton bone 'skewer-pins' and polished stone maceheads were found at both sites. Until the recent discovery of a contemporary cremation cemetery at Ronaldsway in the Isle of Man, and of these Dorchester cemeteries, the practice of cremation was thought to have been an introduction of the Bronze Age. But it is now known to be of much greater antiquity, and its origin must be sought either in indigenous invention in these islands, in some way connected with the Ronaldsway cemetery, or elsewhere. At Er Lannic in Brittany two half-submerged stone circles exist, many of the stones having stone-lined cists at their bases in which were cremations and ritual deposits. These included stone axes and pottery vessels of the *vase-support* type ornamented with dotted triangles and lozenges of the style which we have seen may have been ancestral to our provincial Rinyo-Clacton ware. It seems not impossible that the practice of cremation, and the setting of cremations or standing stones in circles may have formed an integral part of a culture represented on both sides of the Channel.

A few anomalous round barrow burials should also be mentioned here. These may, however, have been derived partly from contact with the contemporary Bell-Beaker and Single-Grave Cultures we have yet to consider. One significant feature not encountered in later barrows of the Bronze Age appears to be the presence of an irregular, pitted, surrounding quarry ditch, sometimes with an entrance causeway as seen in barrows on Handley and Crichel Downs in Dorset, seemingly allied to the ditches of the henge and cursus type. In other instances, the inclusion of perforated antler maceheads of typical Mesolithic ancestry, such as those from barrows on Cop Head Hill, Warminster and at Collingbourne Ducis (with a Group I stone hammer), are almost certainly diagnostic; but it is only when we meet with an assemblage of objects such as those from the Upton Lovel barrow opened by W. Cunnington in 1801, that we can indeed be a little more sure of our ground. Plate 13
This barrow covered a grave in which were two inhumations associated with more than five dozen perforated bone points, very probably used as a fringe to a garment, three flint axes, some mullers of Cornish origin (Groups I and IIIA), two perforated stone battle-axes (one coming from the Whin Sill of the Teesdale area), boars' tusks, a jet ring, jet and bone beads, a bronze awl and a grooved whetstone. Such a mixed group implies an early native burial at a time when the Wessex Bronze Age was just beginning.

Chapter VI

Invasion

Amongst these communities of economically self-sufficient Secondary Neolithic stock-breeders and huntsmen, who were now spreading and multiplying throughout Britain, there appeared on our eastern and southern shores a new immigration round about 1800 B.C., by infiltration no doubt at first, but later to assume considerable proportions. For many years the general characters of these predominantly round-headed invaders, the so-called Beaker-Folk, have been identified both by their characteristic physical form and by their well-made pottery of drinking-vessel or beaker shape decorated with cord or, more usually, hyphenated or fine comb-tooth ornament, and which may connote heavy drinking habits. Physically they were of Dinaric type, large-headed with rugged features, prominent brow-ridges and wide lower jaws, the result, according to Coon, of partial fusion with the Corded-ware people of the Middle Rhineland. But their chief title to fame rests on their introduction of radically different burial customs—individual burial, often under round barrows, and with grave-goods disposed around the body for use in an after-life. This insistence on individualism appears in fact to be their key-note.

Starting, it is usually thought, from Spain, the Bell-Beaker styles of pottery were adopted widely in Europe. Peoples using such pots moved up the western coasts to Brittany and the Channel Islands, and in the Rhineland and Central Europe mixed with other Late Neolithic groups. From the Rhineland and Holland they began to migrate to Britain. In spite of absorption of other traditions and admixture with other cultures, their characteristic vessels of usually bright red ware remained remarkably uniform throughout their progress and

Plates 14, 15, 22

can be recognized almost anywhere. Although contacts with more advanced societies had made them familiar with the advantages of metal, it is essential to recognize in Britain, especially during the early stages of colonization, that these people were primarily a stone-using and sub-Neolithic people who, at the same time, showed no traces of a Mesolithic background. In the past it has been usual to treat them as having ushered in the Early Bronze Age, but it is now very much open to question whether they can any longer command that status and whether their culture was in any way based on that of a metal economy. It cannot be denied that very occasionally they sought and acquired metal articles for ornament and use, but it would be more accurate to class them formally as Late Neolithic with the proviso that they stood on the threshold of the Bronze Age. In Wessex, their close association with, and acceptance of the ways of life of, the Peterborough and Rinyo-Clacton peoples cannot be denied. In fact, they soon seem to have assumed the position of a dominant minority capable of harnessing local resources and of imposing a measure of unification on the existing population, but not until they had contributed substantially to the mixed traditions of the Late Neolithic for several generations at least.

The Beaker invasion was no simple matter; immigrant bands from the Continent entered our eastern and southern shores at numerous points and spread rapidly inland in much the same way as the later Saxon invaders. As long ago as 1912, Lord Abercromby, following Thurnam's original classification of 1871, divided the pottery types introduced by these invaders into two main classes, his so-called A and B Beakers; but it was not until 1929-31 that Professors Childe and Clark gave substance to these two alphabetically termed forms and defined clearly the dual character of the invasion. They were able to show that whereas the A form with its globular body and straight neck was frequently associated with stone battle- Plates 16, 24

axes, flint daggers, barbed and tanged arrow-heads, V-perforated buttons and riveted metal knives or daggers, the B form
Plates 14, 15, 22 of sinuous ovoid outline was usually found with archer's wristguards, similar flint arrow-heads and tanged metal daggers. At the same time, a study of their distribution suggested that the A form had been brought to our eastern shores mainly round the Wash with subsequent penetration overland to Wessex, and that the B form (apparently characteristic of an earlier immigration) was concentrated mainly on our south-eastern and southern coasts, subsequently spreading inland up both the Thames and the Hampshire Avon valleys to the same region. Abercromby's C type beakers can now be seen to represent a third immigration from the Netherlands to north-east England and east Scotland.

Although this dual invasion in its broadest aspects is still recognized, more recent work by Professor Piggott has clarified and at the same time emphasized its complexity. No longer can we accept the implied priority of the A form of beaker but must probably view it as a purely insular development associated with invaders of 'Battle-Axe' tradition who had emanated from the Elbe district of northern Europe. Two distinct points of departure are in fact now admitted as contributing to the components of the Beaker Culture in southern England; an earlier migration from the Rhineland, and a later and perhaps more warlike invasion from the 'Battle-Axe' regions of the Elbe. Both share the custom of Single Grave burial, usually under a barrow.

The B Beaker is the earlier of the two components with which we are here concerned, and most closely approximates to the Bell-Beakers of the Continent, whereas the shape and decoration of the A Beakers form no part of the original complex. With very good reason, therefore, an attempt is being made to drop this somewhat non-informative terminology and, instead, to focus attention on the primary B form by calling it uncompromisingly a Bell-Beaker to indicate its proximate Continental origin, even though regional variants appear as a result of transmarine migration; and to call the A form a Necked Beaker, a term that is sufficiently non-committal and yet retains a clear picture of its essential shape.

BELL-BEAKERS

Bell-Beakers first make their appearance in these islands in late Windmill Hill times when, during the construction of the Giant's Hill long barrow at Skendleby in Lincolnshire, sherds were actually incorporated in the material of the mound. The ware continued in use throughout the Late Neolithic period, and in a few instances has been found to antedate Necked Beakers.

Our knowledge of the people who made them is derived largely from burials in individual graves often, but not always, under a small, circular, low mound or cairn 2 feet or less high; sometimes inserted as secondary burials in existing long barrows as at Thickthorn, and sometimes placed at the foot of standing stones as in the Avebury avenue. The body was invariably placed in a fully contracted position on its side, with a beaker or other articles disposed around. Thus, on the top of Stockbridge Down two small lonely graves were found, one without covering mound but containing a flexed female skeleton with a crudely made beaker, the other just over 100 yards away under a low flint cairn 18 inches high. A young woman whose skeleton suggested a graceful figure and who was of about 25 years of age had been buried under the latter in a grave 3 feet 6 inches deep with a beaker and small bronze awl. Interesting features of this burial were the presence of the surrounding causewayed ditch and of two contemporary cremations that had been placed in the grave whilst it was being *Fig. 6* filled in, both indicative of local Secondary Neolithic practices. Plates 58, 59 An interment which had been inserted later at the edge of the cairn belonged to the Wessex Culture.

Some score or so of such poorly furnished burials are known in Wessex, scattered generally as might befit nomadic life. Probably the most richly furnished graves of the period are those from Mere, Roundway and Winterslow, all in Wiltshire. Plates 14, 15 Each contained, besides beakers of Rhenish form, tanged metal daggers and archer's wristguards, whilst that at Mere had Plate 18 two Irish gold discs, and Roundway a broken metal pin of possibly central European Aunjetitz origin. The daggers are well-known types and are widely distributed from Iberia to Czechoslovakia and the Rhine; but all three possess well defined grooves along the edges of their blades which may mean that they were traded in an unfinished state for later sharpening by those acquiring them. In Britain, such daggers are most likely of Irish origin.

The practice of trepanning the human skull is an old one in prehistoric Europe, and primitive surgery saw fit to indulge in the operation for ritual purposes roughly between 1900 and 1400 B.C. The skull of the dismembered body from the Maiden Castle long mound, previously noted, was so operated upon, and another interesting case comes from a Bell-Beaker Plate 20 grave on Crichel Down, Dorset. Here the roundel of bone had been most skilfully removed by grooving, probably by means of a flint flake, until it could be prised off, the patient meanwhile presumably having been rendered unconscious by some means or another. There is evidence that in a number of instances the patient recovered and that there was growth of new bone; but in this case the operation was unsuccessful.

This practice naturally raises another form of contemporary ritual, that of the ceremonial burial of the head alone, termed cephalotaphy, which may have been resorted to as a charm to increase productivity. In the centre of the Beaker settlement

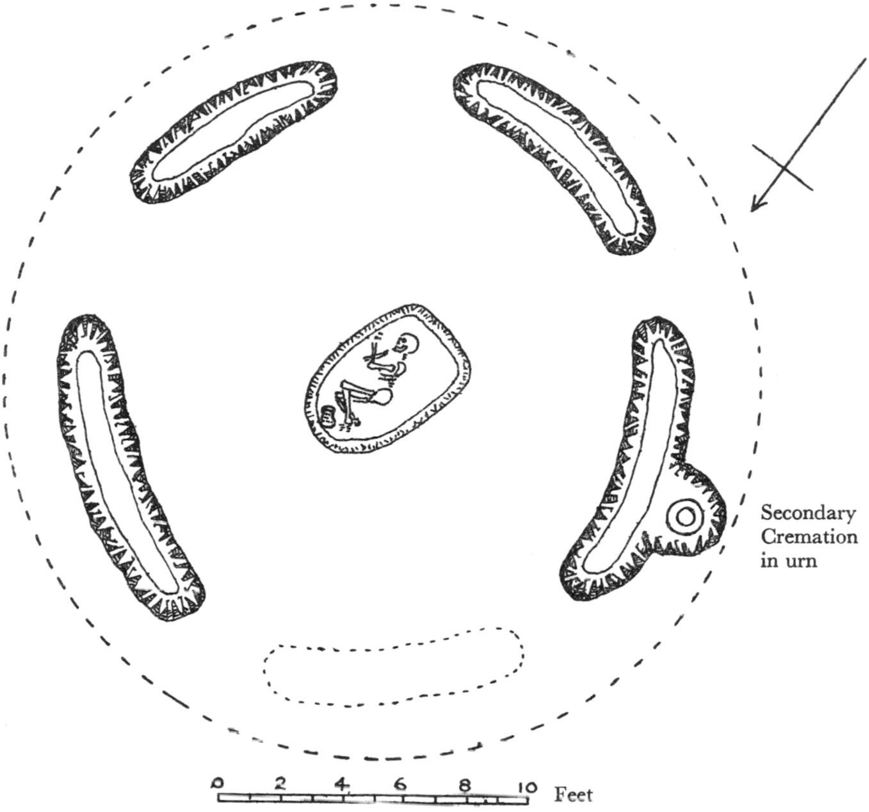

Fig. 6 Plan of Beaker burial under barrow on Stockbridge Down, Hants

surrounding the Easton Down flint-mines is a small barrow 23 feet in diameter and less than 2 feet high. The large grave below was found on excavation to contain a skull only, with atlas and axis articulated, pillowed on 6 inches of chalk dust, and with a roughly chipped bar of flint suggestive of a phallus standing upright against it. This remarkable burial recalls the little altar at the bottom of one of the mine shafts at Grime's

Plate 19

Graves on which was seated the carved representation of a fat pregnant woman with a chalk phallus and antler picks grouped around, no doubt for the same purpose of ensuring a continued supply of good workable flint.

Permanent settlements of the period are rare, but sherds of Beaker ware turn up in many scattered places. The Easton Down flint-mines have so far produced the largest number of pits surrounded by stake holes which have been interpreted as the temporary dwellings of miners and their families who had resorted to the site to replenish their stocks of axes. Beaker sherds of both Bell and Necked varieties are here abundant, accompanied by the refuse of meals and numerous flint implements including scrapers, axes and knives. Under the floor of one of the huts, and at the bottom of a circular pit filled with powdered bone ash, a pet dog had been carefully buried in an attitude of sleep. This dog is of the same large fox-terrier breed

Plate 23

(Canis palustris) as those we have encountered at Windmill Hill and Maiden Castle.

A similar dwelling pit filled with the same sort of domestic rubbish has been recorded from Boscombe Down East, a mile to the north of the flint-mines, and numerous sherds were found in trenching operations on the Larkhill ranges during the last war. At Lymore near Milford-on-Sea, a pit containing nothing but a beaker has been probably erroneously described as a dwelling, though numbers of sherds and somewhat degenerate-looking vessels in the Bournemouth area attest occupation thereabouts.

Whether originally sepulchral or not, two vessels from Inkpen in Berkshire call for special comment. A fine example of a tall Bell-Beaker was here accompanied by an open dish standing on four small legs or feet, which is a type of contemporary

Plates 21, 22

vessel very much favoured in the central European provinces and which may well have been brought over from that region. From that region, too, came fragments of Niedermendig lava brought over possibly for use as quern stones for grinding cereals. This particular form of lava can only have come from the Andernach district of the Rhine; yet pieces have been found in Stonehenge, in the ceremonial site called the Sanctuary near Avebury, and on the line of the Avebury avenue itself.

The crops grown show a marked change from the agricultural habits of the Windmill Hill farmers. From grain impressions on pottery we find that the Beaker-Folk grew principally barley instead of wheat, which is consistent with our knowledge of the same people's habits on the Continent. Whether this was connected with the brewing of strong liquors we do not know, but we may suspect it. The large number of flax seed impressions on a Bell-Beaker from Handley Down in Dorset is also of interest. Such a find is unparalleled in Britain and it is obvious that much seed must have been lying around when the pot was made. This again indicates connexions with the Upper or Middle Rhineland; but at Handley we do not know whether the seed was used as a cereal or for making textiles. Unfortunately we know nothing of the clothing of the Beaker people.

NECKED BEAKERS

Not long after the users of Bell-Beakers from the Rhineland had established an early but firm foothold, other invaders, perhaps of a more warlike nature, from north-eastern Germany may have followed in their footsteps, whose main impact on our shores was between the Wash and Flamborough Head. The stone battle-axes of north European type which suggest the incursion of their users are spread widely from Yorkshire and East Anglia into Derbyshire and Wessex, and are found buried as 'weapons of prestige' in men's graves. Such graves contain objects which relate to the so-called Warrior Cultures of the Battle-Axe,

Single-Grave and Corded-Ware peoples of northern Germany round the Elbe; at the same time, they show insular variations due no doubt to transmarine migration and possibly also to lack or shortage of women-folk amongst the primary invading forces.

This lack can possibly be inferred in Britain from their characteristic pottery vessels, which may be termed Necked Beakers rather than 'Type A', which have no precise Continental parallels, and which are only explicable on the assumption that they were modelled on the lines of the otherwise unrelated Corded-Beakers of the invaders' homeland; for these, though ornamented with cord impressions also possess globular bodies with tall straight necks. The invaders on arrival soon found the country occupied by Bell-Beaker users, with whom they had already been in contact on the Rhineland, and it seems not unnatural that by admixture and intermarriage their insistent demand for vessels of traditional form resulted in the development of this purely insular Necked form combining both the shape and ornament of the two separate forms of Corded- and Bell-Beakers. However, both Bell and Necked Beakers seem to have co-existed since they have been found together in Wick Barrow, Stogursey in Somerset; and that their makers did not clash with the Secondary Neolithic inhabitants, but soon contrived to live with and probably dominate them, seems clear from the way in which sherds of their pottery are so frequently found associated with Peterborough and Rinyo-Clacton types. Occasional hybrid beakers possessing finger-nail or even *pointillé* ornament are evidence of fusion of traditions.

The warlike equipment of these people included stone battle-axes, flint daggers and riveted metal daggers. Sometimes, but not often, these weapons were buried with their dead together with Necked Beakers; more frequently, however, pottery vessels were excluded. It is in fact becoming more and more apparent that many other graves without beakers, but including one or more of these weapons, must represent the British counterparts of these intrusive cultures. Though normally shallow, their single-graves can be very deep; thus one at Wilsford in Wiltshire and another on Crichel Down in Dorset were both nearly 10 feet below ground level. The graves were usually covered by simple bowl barrows, often

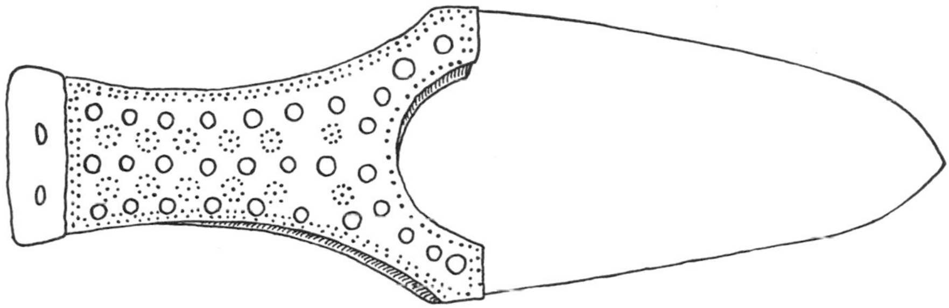

Fig. 7 Bronze knife-dagger with ornamental wooden hilt of rivets and pins of bronze, from burial at Milston, Wilts. $8\frac{1}{4}$ in. overall

much larger than those covering Bell-Beakers, being anything from 5 to 10 feet high and up to 100 feet in diameter.

The stone battle-axes, perforated to take a shaft, are usually simple but finely made with rounded butt and without expanded cutting edge—an insular development of the more complicated Continental forms. They were often made from highly polished and beautiful rocks such as the red tourmaline granite Cornish specimen from Woodhenge and that of olive-green quartzite from Ratfyn nearby. Another large specimen from Fifield Bavant is of preselite, as are others from South Wales, which proves contact again with Pembrokeshire. In fact, the appearance of perforated battle-axes, amongst the products of the Cornish and South Welsh axe factories only clearly shows their interest in these industries and the results of Plate 12 the demands made upon them. The presence of numerous Necked Beaker sherds round the flint-mine shafts of Easton Down and Martin's Clump denotes continued dependence on flint as a raw material for domestic and other purposes; the small scrapers and knives, and barbed and tanged arrow-heads recovered from their temporary shelters are certainly most competently made by pressure flaking which we would hardly expect from any but primary stone-using communities.

The beautifully made thin flint daggers, flaked over both faces, are a case in point, though it cannot be denied that they were probably made to imitate contemporary metal types. They appear in relatively large numbers in East Anglia and the Lower Thames where metal forms are extremely scarce, whereas in Wessex the reverse is the case, which strongly suggests that trade with Irish metallurgists was adequate for their requirements. However, it must not be supposed that copper and bronze daggers of the flat round-heeled riveted type were readily available in Wessex; actually they seem to have been comparatively rare and were probably much prized when acquired. The type is widely distributed throughout Early Bronze Age Europe and it is not easy to determine whence the Wessex specimens came; some may have been brought in by the invaders, but it is more than likely that the majority were obtained through trade with Ireland and were ultimately of Iberian inspiration. Future spectrographic analysis may help to solve the problem. An example of a very rare but
Fig. 7 distinctive British dagger was found early last century at Milston in Wiltshire. Here the handle consisted of two plates of wood held together by thirty bronze rivets and strengthened at the end by a bone pommel. Further, it was decorated by dots in the form of lines and rosettes made by inserted bronze pins. This remarkable piece is clearly related to the gold-studded and gold-mounted dagger-hafts of the later Wessex Culture and can well have been ancestral to them.

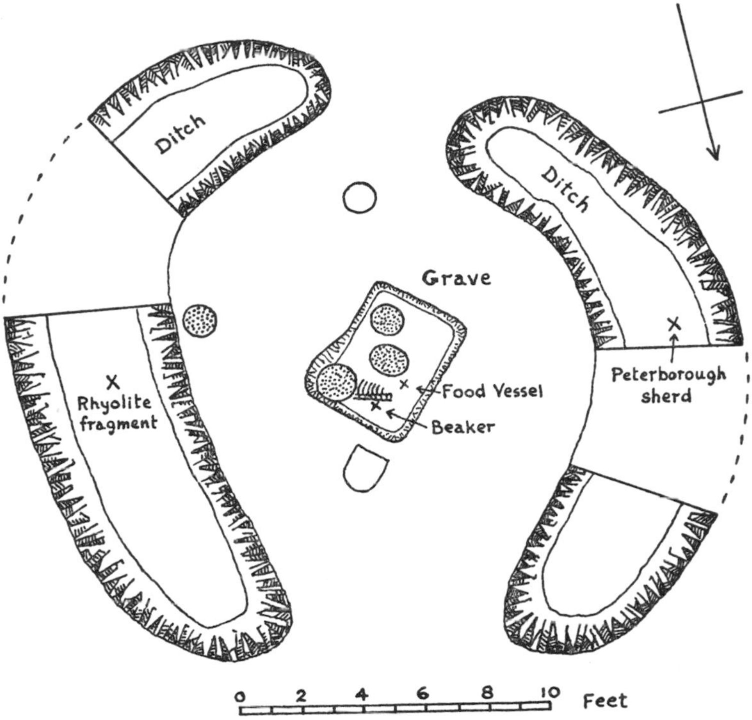

Fig. 8 Burials at Fargo Plantation, Wilts

One of the most difficult problems of this period relates to the status of the early 'Food Vessel' class of pottery occasionally found associated in graves with Necked Beakers. Do they represent a new ethnic element? Are they in their inception an integral part of the Warrior Culture? Or can they be a purely local phenomenon, a development in fact of some of the Secondary Neolithic wares we have already encountered? In the north, various forms of similar pots are relatively abundant and were probably developed from Late Neolithic ceramics with Beaker infusion. Feminine articles such as jet necklaces, copper and bronze awls and small metal knives frequently accompany them, and it has therefore not unnaturally been suggested that some of the earlier examples may represent the female counterparts of the Necked Beakers.

But in the south, and in Wessex in particular, early Food Vessels are exceedingly rare. Two specimens of much the same type have, however, been found actually with Necked Beakers in Fargo Plantation, three-quarters of a mile north-west of Stonehenge, and on Charmy Down near Bath. No barrow covered the Fargo grave, which was 3 feet deep; but in it and sealed in by a compact layer of chalk rubble were the beaker and food vessel, a partial inhumation consisting of the upper part of a body only, without head, and two cremations. All were undoubtedly contemporary. The ditch with its two wide causeways surrounding the grave presents points of considerable interest; here we have a very small example of a type of ceremonial earthwork known technically as a 'henge', such as we associate with the Beaker-Folk, and which will be examined in the next chapter. A deep post-hole just inside the southern entrance may well have held some form of totem-pole; whilst in the ditch was a fragment of the Pembrokeshire bluestone rhyolite and a large sherd of Peterborough pottery, the bearing of which on Blue Stonehenge we shall mention later. The Charmy Down beaker and food vessel were associated with a small bronze riveted knife-dagger and a ribbed bead of shale, a type of bead that normally accompanies the grave-goods of the immediately succeeding Wessex Culture and which clearly suggests cultural overlap.

Plates 24, 25

Fig. 8

Unfortunately we know all too little of the mode of life of these warriors. Conical shale buttons with V-perforations and grooved shale belt rings or fastenings imply more advanced forms of clothing, though traces of textiles have been recorded only once—from a Beaker burial at Kellythorpe in Yorkshire. To visualize garments from a few buttons only is, however, beyond our capability, though we note in passing that button-fastened garments in early second millennium Europe are characteristically western, as opposed to those fastened by decorative pins which are distinctive of central and northern Europe.

CHAPTER VII

Temples

OUT OF THE COMPLEX amalgam of differing ethnic and cultural groups we have so far considered there arose a distinctive manifestation of the Late Neolithic period, the construction of ritual or ceremonial circular enclosures known as 'henges'. Their origin is shrouded in obscurity though we do know that they are confined solely to Great Britain and have no Continental parallels or prototypes from which they could have sprung. The word 'henge' is, strictly speaking, applicable to Stonehenge only in its final form with superimposed stone lintels as a name meaning 'the stone gallows'. But by common usage, following Sir Thomas Kendrick's original definition of this class of monument in 1932, and in the absence of a more suitable word, the term is now generally applied to various roughly contemporary enclosures having certain features in common. These features normally consist of a surrounding bank and ditch, with the ditch *inside* the bank as opposed to other earthworks of clearly defensive character, and with one or more causewayed entrances. The areas so enclosed,
Fig. 8 which may vary in diameter from only 20 feet as in the Fargo
Fig. 15 Plantation grave to over 1500 feet in the case of Durrington Walls, may, but do not always, include circles of upright
Figs. 11, 12, 14 stones (Avebury and Stonehenge II) or timber posts (Woodhenge), or of ritual holes or pits which have been demonstrated never to have held either (Stonehenge I), or even of one or more burials only (Fargo Plantation).

With only a few exceptions practically all these earthworks appear to have been carefully sited on level, often low-lying,
Fig. 9 ground frequently in relatively close proximity to streams or rivers; the enclosed areas are clearly visible from the encircling banks, which appear to have been the most important feature,

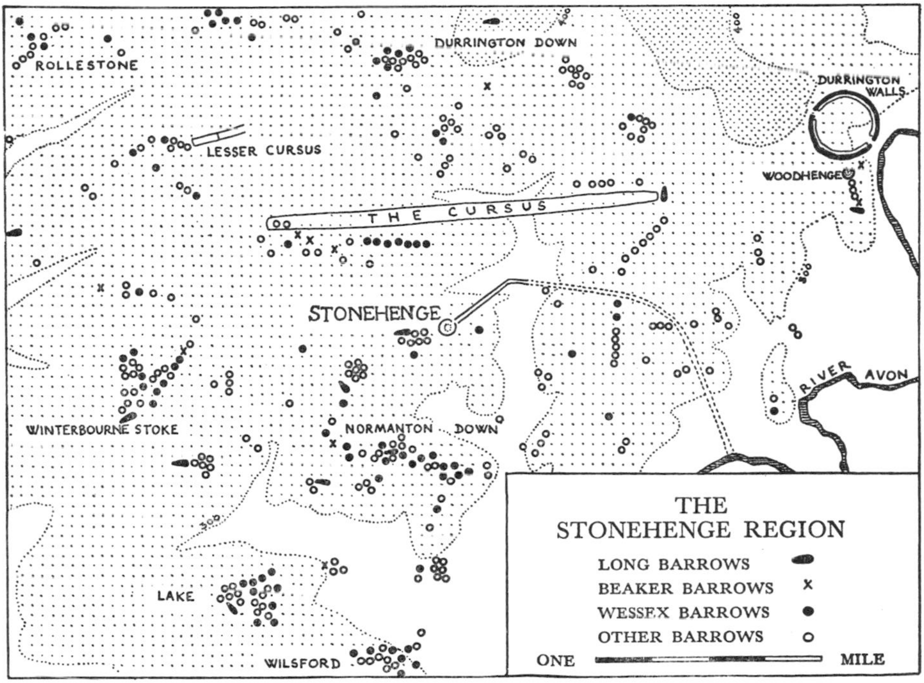

Fig. 9 Barrow-burials around Stonehenge

the ditch having been a mere quarry whence the material for their construction was obtained. Avenues of stones or earthen banks in some instances lead to or from them. Plate 27

Some forty-five or fifty monuments of the class have been recognized within recent years, distributed from Cornwall to the Orkney Islands. Probably a good fifteen of them of every possible combination lie in Wessex alone, though not all have been tested by excavation. In spite, however, of very considerable variation, attempts have been made to divide them into two classes, those with a single entrance having been ascribed to the earlier Secondary Neolithic phase, and those with two or more to the later Beaker Cultures. This division is broadly true though it cannot be accepted yet as invariable and much more work needs to be done on these sites; cultural overlapping undoubtedly took place, whilst under Beaker domination many of our finest examples appear to have been constructed, especially those embodying standing stones as at Avebury. This is important as emphasizing the acceptance and adoption by the Beaker-Folk and Warrior Cultures of some of the ceremonial practices initiated locally by the non-Beaker elements of the population. The introduction of the single-grave under a round barrow by these intruders completely inhibited, as we have seen, the rite of communal burial under long barrows; yet for some unknown reason the ceremonial henge found favour and under Beaker influence and organization expanded to remarkable lengths. The nature of the ceremonies and rites enacted in them we shall never know, but it is certain, as R. J. C. Atkinson has pointed out, that the beliefs which found expression in such a building as that of Avebury must have been of a peculiarly compelling kind. Although it is agreed that the majority were regarded as sacred and non-utilitarian in character, there is no reason to suppose that their primary function was necessarily sepulchral or connected with acts of worship of some primitive deity. A few may have been used as tribal assembly places whilst others, *Fig. 8* like the small Fargo Plantation grave, may simply be anomalous graves built on the lines of the larger and more formal 'temples'. However, the existence of cremation cemeteries within some of them and the number of barrows that surround others both strongly argue in favour of the supposition that some at least were connected with a cult of the dead.

Stonehenge and Avebury, our two most famous examples, Plates 26–29, 32 lie on the Wiltshire Downs at nodal points on the waterways and transpeninsular routes which were to contribute to the rise of Wessex to power. Although both are atypical, it is appropriate that we should consider them first; but it should not be forgotten that in their strategic positions they not unnaturally underwent a number of periods of reconstruction and development which have added considerably to the difficulties of archæological interpretation and masked their underlying unity.

STONEHENGE I

As a result of recent excavations carried out since 1950, it has became increasingly clear that Stonehenge had a long history, which must be divided into at least three major periods of construction. In his recent book on Stonehenge, R. J. C. Atkinson has considered the monument in great detail and it is, therefore, unnecessary to recapitulate the mass of evidence and its interpretation which he has so ably assembled and reviewed. I shall endeavour here merely to confine myself to a few points of outstanding interest.

It will be recalled that Stonehenge lies in an area of Secondary Neolithic settlement, and that the undressed monolith, the Heel Stone, *may* represent the earliest feature on the site. This is certainly suggested by the fact that, at some date later than at the time of its erection, an Early Bronze Age beaker had been broken against it, the fragments of which were found during the excavations, having slipped down the side of the stone as it canted over due to the rotting of anti-friction stakes at its base. However, it is now generally agreed that the first major period of construction, that of Stonehenge I, consisted of the digging of the Ditch and Bank and the Aubrey Holes. These features were laid out with considerable accuracy in true circles from the same centre, the diameter of the Bank being about 320 feet. The flat-based quarry Ditch, in this instance on the *outside* of the Bank, has almost vertical sides and averages 5½ feet in depth. One functional causeway 35 feet wide was left as an entrance, and early excavations by Colonel *Fig. 10*

Hawley revealed numerous post-holes of unknown significance over its surface. Besides antler picks and rough flint implements, the only objects of importance so far recovered from the primary silting of the Ditch have been four or five sherds of
Fig. 5 Rinyo-Clacton ware, which are comparable with those from Woodhenge nearby and can be dated about 1900-1700 B.C.

The fifty-six Aubrey Holes, originally discovered by John Aubrey in 1666, are set in a circle just within the Bank and, when rediscovered in the early 1920s, were supposed to have held originally stone or timber uprights. Later excavations in 1950, coupled with the discovery of similar pits in other henges at Dorchester near Oxford and on Cairnpapple Hill in West Lothian, showed that they were not structural in function but must have been connected with some ritual or cult of which we now have no knowledge. The holes are roughly circular pits varying from about 2 to 4 feet in depth and contain very mixed fillings of chalk rubble, burnt material and soil. Many seem to have been deliberately refilled soon after digging; others, having been filled were redug to varying depths and fresh deposits were placed in them. Small heaps of cremated human bones have been found in most of the thirty-two that have so far been examined; but this need not imply that the holes were originally sepulchral, since other cremations have been found in the Ditch and under the turf just within the Bank.

About fifty-five cremations have been found in this flat cemetery, one of which was actually on the floor of the Ditch with no signs of disturbance above, which shows that it was contemporary. Long skewer-like bone pins, flint bars or fabricators, a small polished stone macehead and a minute pottery vessel accompanied some of them. Such objects are characteristic of the Secondary Neolithic cultures in Britain, as are also six Cornish stone axes from the site. By good fortune sufficient charcoal was obtained from Aubrey Hole 32 for a

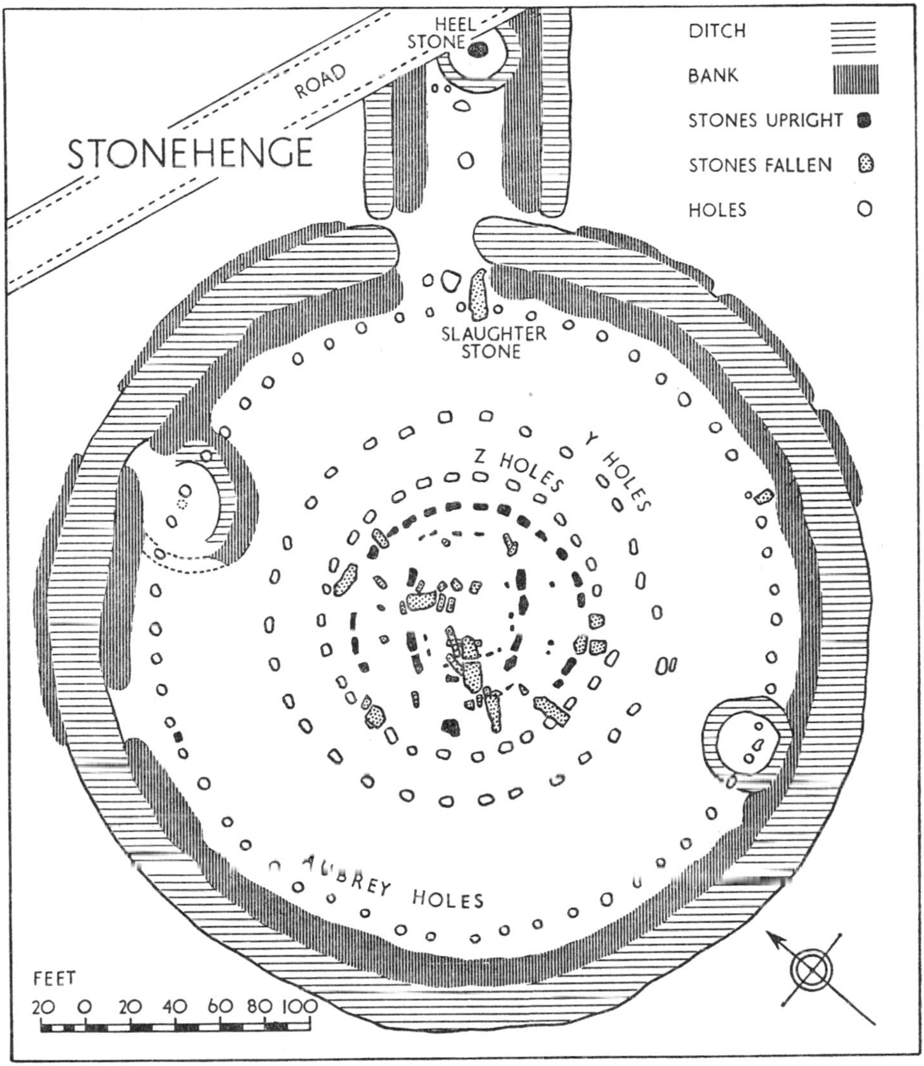

Fig. 10 Plan of Stonehenge as at present

radio-active carbon analysis of date by W. F. Libby of Chicago. This yielded 1848 B.C. ± 275 years, which means that the odds are about 2 to 1 that Stonehenge I was constructed between 2125 and 1575 B.C. Admittedly the margin of uncertainty here is great but, nevertheless, this C14 analysis does support the date of 1900-1700 B.C., arrived at independently by archæological means. It should be added that no evidence exists for any contemporary internal structure.

STONEHENGE II

This structure no longer exists and is completely invisible to the ordinary visitor. Its very presence was unsuspected until 1954, when excavations within the monument on the line of the existing but robbed and defaced bluestone circle were carried out to determine the spacing of this last and latest circle. These disclosed the settings of an earlier double circle with diameters of 74 and 86 feet respectively and of about thirty-eight stones apiece; however, the stones had been extracted at a later date for purposes of reconstruction. Each adjacent pair of 'Q' and 'R' holes formed the ends of dumb-bell-shaped hollows tightly packed with chalk rubble where the stones had once stood, with minute fragments of bluestones embedded in them. Clear evidence was thus obtained that a Blue Stonehenge had preceded the erection of the present monument. The entrance to this double circle, marked by two additional inlying pairs of stone-holes, is not aligned on the causeway of Stonehenge I, but on that of the axis of the present structure. This most important fact proves that the orientation on the midsummer sunrise was deliberate, and that very probably the construction of the Avenue was conceived at the same time. *Fig. 11;* Plate 31

The relative date of Stonehenge II has been shown to lie between the end of Stonehenge I and the erection of the sarsen

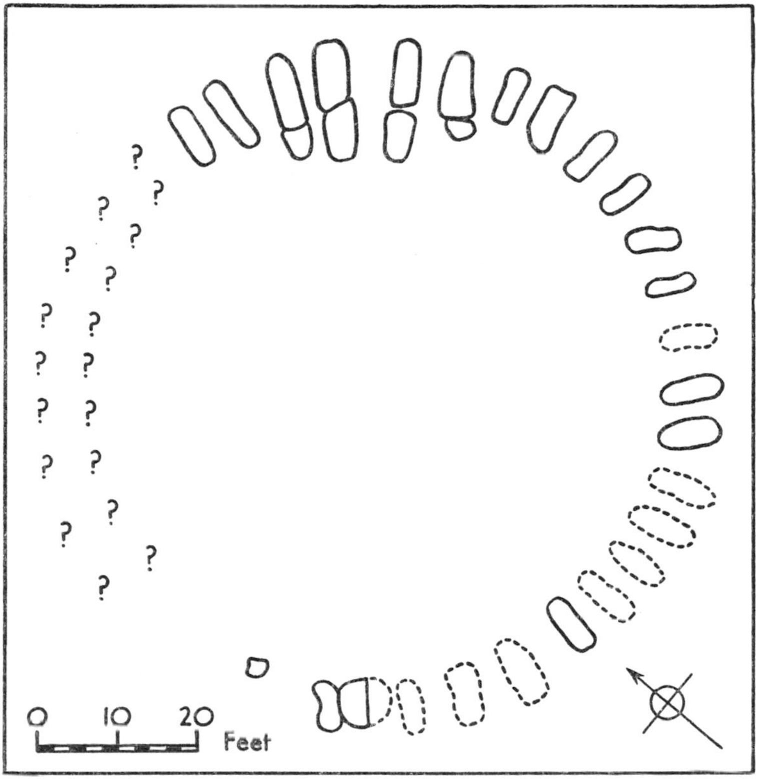

Fig. 11 Plan of stone-holes representing the monument of Stonehenge II

structure. This corresponds with the position of bluestone fragments and Beaker pottery in the Ditch on top of the secondary silting. Hence it has been inferred that the period of its construction must lie around 1700-1600 B.C.

But the building was never completed. The most surprising fact that emerged from continued excavations in 1956 was that a part of the western quadrant, as yet of unknown extent, was devoid of any traces of these double stone-holes. If, as seems likely, a double circle of undressed bluestone monoliths was conceived under Beaker dominance, the project was abandoned when only three-quarters completed. This may have been due to a variety of causes; the supply of the required number of stones from Pembrokeshire may have temporarily stopped; the decision to dismantle another possible bluestone circle in the vicinity (for such may have existed at the west end of the Cursus) and to add its stones to the quota may have been abandoned; or a new decision may have been taken under foreign influence to build the grandiose structure we know today. I propose to consider this later Stonehenge III phase in a subsequent chapter.

Nevertheless, the fact remains that the stones, each weighing upwards of 4 tons, were brought from Pembrokeshire, a distance of 135 miles as the crow flies, and from the same restricted area of the Prescelly Mountains from which the Beaker-Folk were deriving their preselite battle-axes. It was in 1923 that H. H. Thomas proved conclusively by petrological analysis that the three main varieties of rocks at Stonehenge, spotted dolerite or preselite, rhyolite and volcanic ash all came from relatively confined areas on the Prescelly Mountains, and that the so-called Altar Stone of micaceous sandstone in all probability came from the Cosheston Beds around Milford Haven. The stump of a block of Cosheston grey-green sandstone and chippings have also been found more recently to have emanated from Mill Bay on the southern shore of the same Haven.

Plate 12

The problem of transport must have been a heavy one; but recent thought and experiment favours a coastal route along the South Welsh coast, on canoes lashed together, with subsequent carriage up the Bristol Avon to Frome and thence overland to the River Wylye at Warminster; and finally down the Wylye to Salisbury and from there to Amesbury. From Amesbury to Stonehenge we have the earth-embanked Avenue connecting the river with the monument; its presence may denote some form of processional way up which the

Fig. 9

sacred stones were dragged on sledges. But even so, many of Plate 30 the stones must have been lost in transit and now lie submerged below sea- and river-level. This Bristol Avon waterway was, as we have seen, a much frequented one, and evidence is accumulating to show that Beaker movements and trade to South Wales and Ireland made use of it. Thus, we have an Irish gold disc from Monkton Farleigh similar to those from Plate 17 Mere, and Beaker graves at Charmy Down and Corston near Plate 18 Bath within easy reach of the unembanked Stanton Drew stone circles with their attendant stone avenues, which in some way were connected with the River Chew, a tributary of the Avon. Here the stones appear to have been hauled some 5 miles from nearby outcrops at Harptree on the Mendips, about 5 miles from which lies Gorsey Bigbury, a somewhat ambiguous henge. This last monument has yielded no evidence of internal features, but from the ditch nearly a hundred fragmentary Necked Beakers and much rusticated ware have been obtained; large numbers of flint implements, including microliths, accompanied them. Brean Down on the Severn has also yielded fragments of the same pottery.

AVEBURY

If sheer size and complexity are criteria, the enormous earthworks and associated stone structures at Avebury on the Marlborough Plates 27, 28, 32 Downs are unquestionably the most impressive monuments of the period in Great Britain. The labour involved must have been immense when we recall that the builders had to rely for tools on wood for levers, rollers and sledges, and on antler picks and scapulæ of oxen for digging and shovelling. But now a very large part of the village of Avebury lies within the huge encircling bank and ditch, and time and the hand of man have mutilated and sadly impaired its former grandeur. It is indeed very difficult to appreciate today at a glance and from any one spot the underlying theme as a whole; yet when we recall that the bank once rose at least 50 feet above the bottom of the wide and flat-based ditch, and that the whole of the enclosed 28½ acres was once embellished with numerous massive stone circles and monoliths (now mostly demolished for building the village) we can vaguely appreciate that we stand in what must have been one of the greatest religious centres of the country.

Fig. 12; Plate 28

The organization of the necessary man-power and the underlying resolve needed for such an astonishing project transcended by far that needed for so relatively small a structure as Stonehenge II; yet there is reason to believe that they were both constructed at about the same time and by the same people.

As long ago as 1648 John Aubrey noted that Avebury far surpassed Stonehenge 'as a cathedral doth a parish church', whilst Stukeley has for ever placed us in his debt by describing and illustrating the monument as he saw it in 1723. Although a number of excavations have since been carried out within it, nothing systematic was attempted until 1908-22 when H. St. G. Gray investigated some areas of the ditch and bank, to be followed by A. Keiller in 1934-39 who was able to throw considerable light on the stone structures themselves and to institute a policy of careful conservation and reconstruction. But it cannot be said that these investigations in so large an area have clarified the history of the monument. They have instead emphasized its complexity and made it more difficult to relate the various components involved. All that can be inferred at present is that the whole monument evolved by slow development within the period of the Secondary Neolithic-Beaker cultural overlap, and that it was not planned in its entirety as one coherent whole.

The vast internal ditch, in places 30 feet deep and as much as 17 feet at the base, is now filled with silt to about 17 feet, and

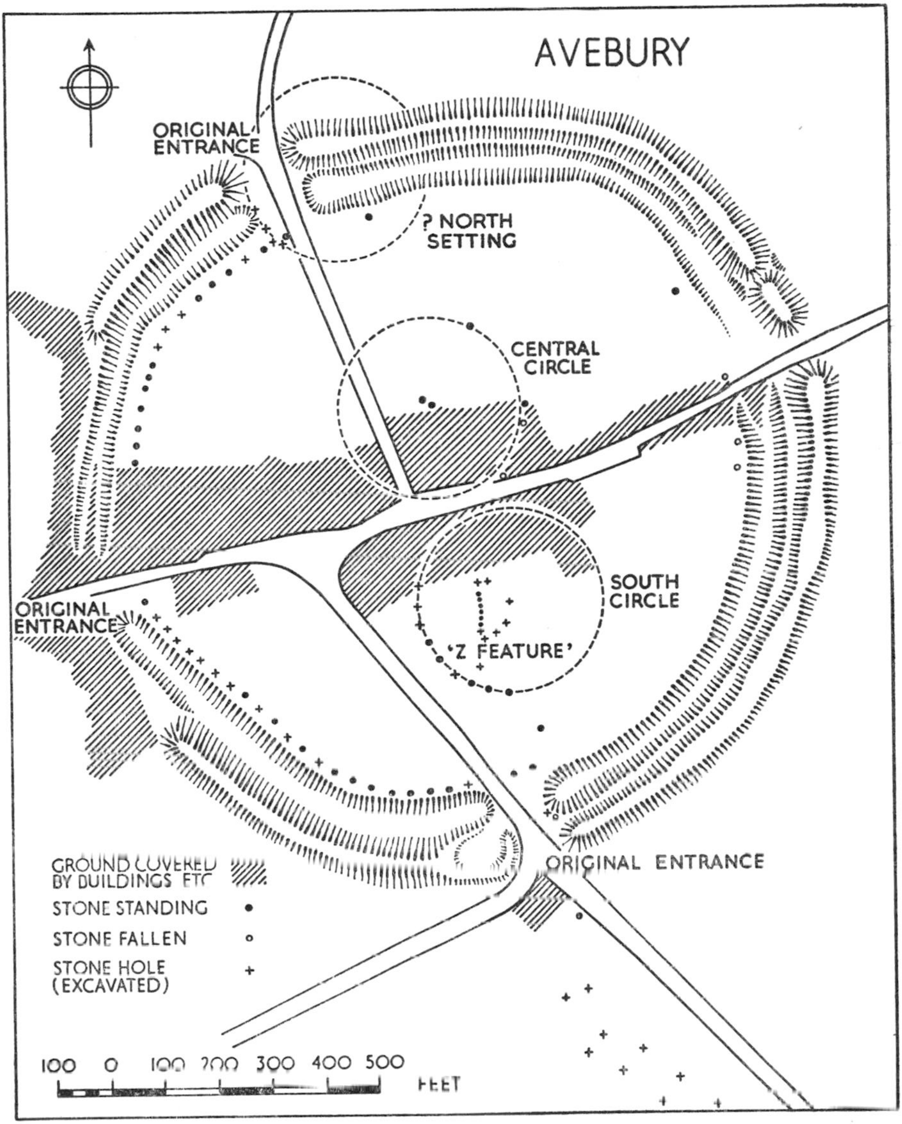

Fig. 12 Plan of Avebury stone circles

Fig. 12 has three proven causeways on the north, south and west, with possibly another on the east. The bank, now about 15 feet high and ¾ mile in circumference, is composed of chalk rubble with a facing or revetment of Lower Chalk blocks which had been obtained from the bottom of the ditch, higher levels consisting of Middle Chalk only. Peterborough ware, *petit tranchet* arrow-heads, flint scrapers and serrated flakes, with blades of polished ox-ribs, have been obtained from the old ground surface beneath it; the secondary silting of the ditch yielded both Peterborough and Beaker sherds, and the burial of a female dwarf surrounded by an oval setting of sarsen blocks. No identifiable sherds have been recovered from the primary silt.

Inside the ditch, and about 30 feet from its edge, stood the Great Stone Circle consisting originally of about a hundred huge sarsen monoliths, a very large pair of which still stand at Plate 28 the entrance to the Avenue. These blocks of sarsen, a highly silicified sedimentary sandstone, still occur in great profusion on the Marlborough Downs, the remains of a local capping of the chalk, and are here known as 'grey-wethers'. The use of packing blocks of Lower Chalk round some of these stones proves that the circle was erected at the time the ditch was dug.

Two smaller circles originally stood inside the Great Stone Circle, the central one comprising some 30 stones set on a diameter of 320 feet with, in the middle, a setting of three closely spaced uprights named by Stukeley a 'Cove' and similar to other settings at Stanton Drew in Somerset. The southern circle, of which only five stones remain, originally held some thirty-two stones set on a diameter of 336 feet, with a central monolith 21 feet high recorded by Stukeley but no longer present. The northern circle, or rather the presence of three stone-holes interpreted as such during the 1934-39 excavations, is unproved and ambiguous; if it really existed before the construction of the bank, ditch and Great Stone Circle, an earlier date could be inferred for these three internal circles. But no evidence exists for independent dating. The line of stone-holes inside the southern circle, known as the Z feature, cannot be interpreted; Lower Chalk blocks were, however, found as packing blocks in the holes.

From the southern entrance the West Kennet Avenue of sarsen monoliths follows a somewhat tortuous rather than sinuous course southwards for a distance of nearly 1½ miles and terminates at another stone and timber building on Overton *Fig. 13*

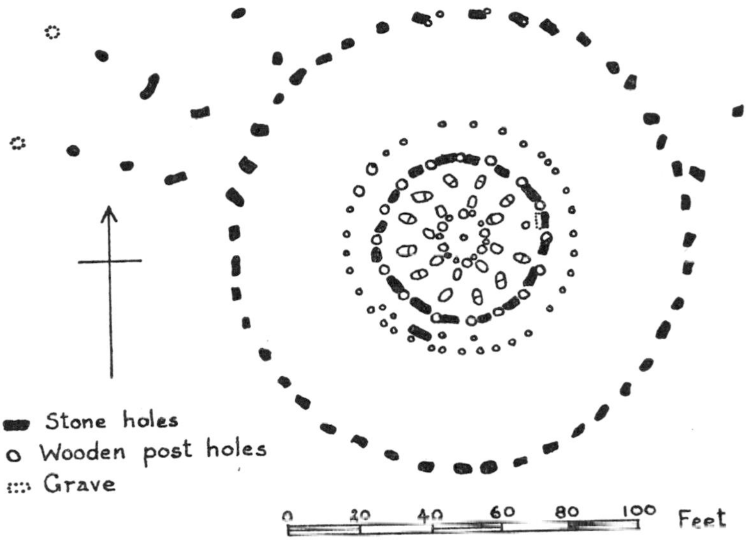

Fig. 13 Plan of the stone and timber circles at The Sanctuary, Avebury, Wilts

Hill known as the Sanctuary. This Avenue consisted originally of about 200 stones set in pairs spaced 80 feet apart longitudinally and 50 feet transversely; and it has been noted that both the Avebury and Sanctuary branches run down to the River Kennet. This can hardly be fortuitous and, since the avenues at Stonehenge and Stanton Drew are also linked directly with rivers, it seems not unlikely that the West Kennet Avenue may once have consisted of two independent parts which later were joined together. Plate 27

Over part of its course the Avenue has been shown to run through a Secondary Neolithic settlement which has yielded typical Peterborough, Rinyo-Clacton and Beaker sherds, as well as Cornish and Graig Lwyd axes and Niedermendig lava. At the bases of three of the stones were burials, two with Bell-Beakers and one with a Rinyo-Clacton bowl.

The Sanctuary has been totally effaced, though it partly existed in Stukeley's day. It was, however, subsequently rediscovered and excavated in 1930 by Mrs. Cunnington who, to perpetuate its memory, marked the positions of the stone and timber post-holes found with low concrete pillars. This small structure is not a simple one; clearly it had been modified and rebuilt a number of times. The earlier feature embodying six concentric timber circles with a single post at the centre very possibly represents the plan of a roofed wooden building 65 feet in diameter which, after periods of reconstruction, was demolished and replaced by the concentric stone circles. The outer one of these consisted of forty-two stones set on a diameter of 130 feet and the inner of thirty-two stones on a diameter of 45 feet. The Kennet Avenue, which narrows as it approaches, is joined to the outer stone circle on the north-west. Peterborough and Beaker sherds were recovered from the post-holes together with *petit tranchet* arrow-heads and Niedermendig lava; the burial of a youth of long-headed, long barrow type about 14 years old, and possibly dedicatory, was found at the base of one of the stones of the inner circle together with a Bell-Beaker.

Fig. 13

Just over a mile to the west of The Sanctuary, and also on the Bath road, lies Silbury Hill, the largest prehistoric artificial mound in Europe, whose volume is approximately $12\frac{1}{2}$ million cubic feet and which covers about $5\frac{1}{2}$ acres. It is now 130 feet high, 550 feet in diameter and has a flat top 100 feet across. Its position in the immediate vicinity of the Avebury complex suggests that it may be contemporary but no evidence exists

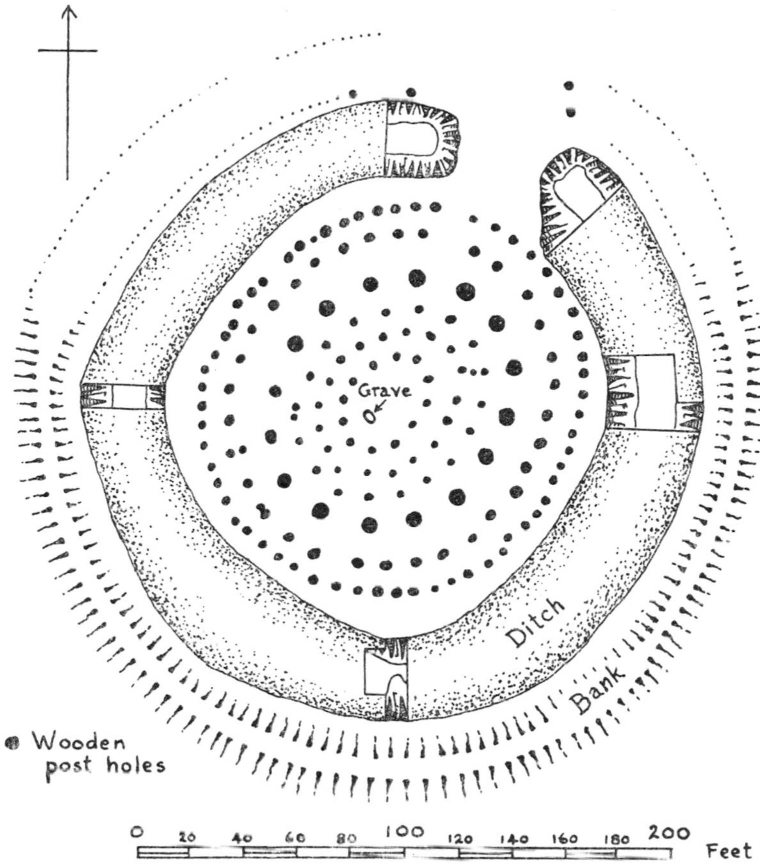

Fig. 14 Plan of Woodhenge, Wilts

whereby to date it other than by the fact that the adjacent Roman road was intentionally diverted to avoid it. A number of attempts by tunnelling and the sinking of shafts have been made to force its secret, but these have proved unsuccessful. Dean Merewether in 1849 found a conical heap of turf with many sarsen boulders near its centre on the old turf line, and records the presence of antler tines and 'fragments of a sort of string, of two strands, each twisted, composed of (as it seemed) grass, and about the size of whipcord'. If really a colossal barrow, it is certainly worthy of its setting in the metropolitan area of Avebury and must form the resting place of someone of very considerable authority and prestige.

WOODHENGE

We have already commented on the evidence of Secondary Neolithic settlement embraced within the Woodhenge-Durrington Walls district. In this relatively small area on the western bank of the River Avon, just over 1 mile north of Amesbury and within 2 miles of Stonehenge, are two contiguous henges of outstanding interest, the relationship of which to each other is by no means clear though both appear to have been in use at the same time.

Fig. 14

Woodhenge was discovered from the air in 1925 by Squadron-Leader G. S. M. Insall, V.C., who noticed rings of black dots within a circular enclosure which until then had mistakenly been thought to be a ploughed-down disc barrow. Subsequent excavations by Mr. and Mrs. Cunnington in 1926-28 proved that these dots were in fact timber post-holes arranged in six concentric circles within a ditched enclosure having one entrance causeway. By analogy with Stonehenge the earthwork was jocularly termed Woodhenge even though no evidence existed for any form of lintelled structure.

This earthwork is from bank to bank 250 feet in diameter with an internal flat-based quarry ditch. In it was an inhumation grave cut into the chalk base before silting began. The post-holes within vary in size, increasing inwards to the third ring which must have held massive timber uprights, the holes for which had ramps and were on an average 5 feet in diameter and 5 feet 8 inches deep. The inner three rings then decrease in

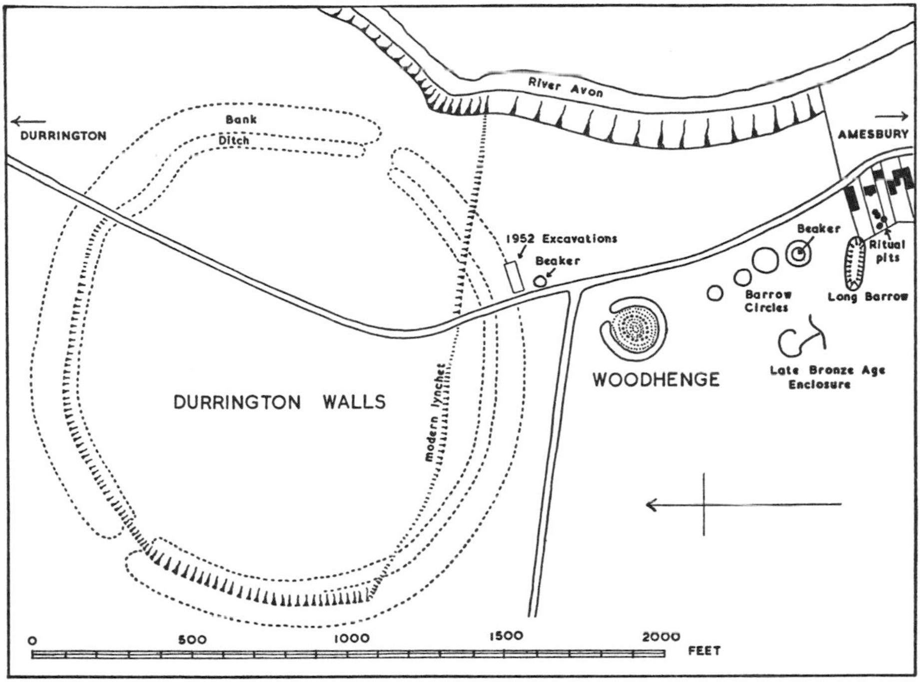

Fig. 15 Plan of Durrington Walls and adjacent monuments, Wilts

size to the centre. The plan suggests no periods of reconstruction; and the building may probably have been roofed with an open centre. Just off centre was a shallow grave containing an infant with skull cleft in half, possibly a sacrificial or dedicatory deposit. One cremation was found in one of the large postholes. Considerable quantities of plastically ornamented Rinyo-Clacton ware occurred in the ditch and under the bank. But Windmill Hill and Beaker sherds occurred too with *petit tranchet* arrow-heads, serrated flakes, scrapers and two ritual chalk axes. This suggests that the building lay in an area of intensive occupation, the stratification of which is by no means clear. As at The Sanctuary, the position of the holes has been marked with concrete pillars.

DURRINGTON WALLS

Another ceremonial henge comparable in size to, and indeed larger than that at Avebury, but lacking evidence of stone or timber uprights, lies within 80 yards of Woodhenge. Durrington Walls unfortunately is now much defaced and almost obliterated, and its huge size is thus difficult to appreciate from the ground. It is of the double entrance type, with one entrance opening directly on to the River Avon, and has been built at the head of a combe, the whole central area of which is visible from the top of any part of the bank. Pipe-laying operations in 1950 disclosed considerable Rinyo-Clacton occupational refuse under the northern bank and similar refuse overlapping the tail of the southern, associated, as we have seen, with some elongated timber structure. A sherd of Beaker ware was, however, found under the western bank in 1917.

Fig. 15

OTHER HENGES

Other henges have been identified in Wessex, but it would be tedious and unnecessary to enumerate them all here. Marden in the Vale of Pewsey may lay claim to being the largest, but we know virtually nothing about it. Maumbury Rings near Dorchester has a single entrance and is remarkable in having a ditch composed of numerous huge conical pits up to 35 feet deep. The double-entrance henge at Knowlton near Cranborne (one of a group of henge and related earthworks) is surprising in possessing, in its extremely isolated position, the ruins of a small twelfth- to sixteenth-century church within its enclosure. This act of consecration of a pagan monument, where certain unlawful acts may well have persisted, should be compared with the intentional defacement and burial of many of the stones of the Avebury circles and avenue in the thirteenth and fourteenth centuries, under one of which was found the crushed skeleton of a barber-surgeon of the time of Edward I; and of the deliberate defacement and destruction of many of the stones at Stonehenge at some unknown but probably post-Roman date.

Another possible enclosure of the Woodhenge type may exist on Silk Hill, Brigmerston, on the opposite side of the Avon and 3 miles north-east of Durrington Walls.

CHAPTER VIII

The Final Stonehenge

IN OUR SUMMARY REVIEW of ceremonial enclosures we have seen that sufficiently stable conditions existed for human resources and manpower to be devoted largely to their construction under Beaker and Warrior Culture dominance. No warrant exists, however, for assuming that any form of kingship over a large area existed; at most, local control must have been exercised by culturally related chieftains acting sometimes in competition, at other times in consort with all the resources at their disposal in the execution of some huge earthwork or stone structure. Small earthworks may conceivably have been connected with temporary halting places or local tribes, but structures of the size and complexity of Avebury point to the existence of some more centralized and permanent authority.

Fig. 10; Plate 26

Both Stonehenge I and II are consistent with this general class of enclosure and stone circle of Secondary Neolithic-Beaker inception, including even the transport of the bluestones which was certainly an outstanding achievement. But Stonehenge III, the last and final structure in this monument's chequered history, does not fall within the class. Instead, it stands out sharply as a completely new and unique feat in north-western Europe, built on a site that involved a very large shift in the centre of gravity from the Marlborough Downs to South Wiltshire, and involving also the transport of colossal blocks of sarsen weighing up to 50 tons apiece from that hallowed district 18 miles to the north. This shift of emphasis will become more apparent when we come to consider, in the next chapter, the Early Bronze Age Wessex Culture and its barrows; but there can be little doubt that it was mainly due to the new and competing factor of the metal trade with Europe, which arose as a direct result of the ready market offered to

Irish metallurgists by the Beaker and sub-Beaker population. Stonehenge, with its avenue to the River Avon, was certainly more advantageously placed on the natural route from the West to the English Channel than was Avebury, and few would question that this new factor proved powerful enough to efface all traces of former self-sufficiency and at the same time the venue of traditional practices; even the less distinguished Woodhenge and Durrington Walls now fell into disuse. Some might wish to connect the rise of Stonehenge with the introduction of sun-worship which we have seen may be presumed to be inherent in the orientation of the Stonehenge II structure; but such speculations are profitless in the absence of exact knowledge.

I have said that Stonehenge III is unique. This is true in that a large number of the sarsens and bluestones have been dressed to shape and finish in a building that also possesses curved lintels poised on their uprights with mortise and tenon jointing, and Plate 36
with tongues and grooves holding them more securely in place, a carpentry technique transferred to stone and far in advance of the mere erection of free-standing boulders. Dishing of the tops of the uprights aided stability, whilst the convexly curved taper or *entasis* on some seems purposely to have been an added refinement. The plan of the sarsen structure is symmetrical and shapely, and it must be clear that the designer was no novice. It is in fact inconceivable that such a structure could have arisen in the North out of the void without some examples of experimental development behind it. Such a unique object postulates a unique event, and I feel sure that we must look to the literate civilizations of the Mediterranean for the inspiration and indeed for the actual execution under the hands and eyes of some trader or mission from that region.

The main problem underlying Stonehenge III is that in its final form it utilized elements from two separate lintelled structures, one of sarsen and the other of bluestone, with possibly a third of undressed bluestone boulders, which were ultimately fused into one building after a considerable amount of reshuffling of the bluestone elements. These Pembrokeshire bluestones include undressed monoliths, presumably derived from the uncompleted Stonehenge II circles, and a number of dressed stones including two lintels which *may* have formed part of the original plan, or which *may* have stood elsewhere in the vicinity, to be incorporated only at a later stage. Recent excavations have been largely concerned in attempts to unravel some of these phases, but it cannot be said that they have met as yet with complete success. It is not, as I have said, my intention to describe the monument in detail as this has been done by my colleague R. J. C. Atkinson. All that I need here emphasize are some of the problems and conclusions we have tentatively arrived at individually and collectively, the most important being that three main building phases have been distinguished, though even here it would be wrong to assume that they are firmly established.

STONEHENGE IIIA

After the total removal of the double bluestone circle from the already hallowed site, the 'Q' and 'R' holes were refilled and packed with chalk rubble. Disregarding the immense problems associated with the transport of the sarsens from the Marlborough Downs and the victualling of the hundreds of workers employed on the project, the first phase must have been concerned with the dressing and erection of the five great trilithons and the outer circle of thirty uprights with their thirty lintels. The fact that the same centre and axis were used suggests no lengthy period of discontinuity between the abortive erection of Stonehenge II and the decision to abandon it in favour of the novel design that somehow now presented itself.

This symmetrical and superlative sarsen structure may be considered to have been complete in itself. No compelling reason can be adduced to suggest that the original plan necessarily contemplated the incorporation of the undressed bluestone boulders; this may well have been an afterthought. Nevertheless, we cannot disregard the fact that other masons at the same time must have been dressing and possibly constructing a smaller imitation with lintels somewhere in the vicinity. It will be recalled that a chipping of rhyolite was found in the ditch of the Fargo Plantation grave three-quarters of a mile to the north-west. It was for that very reason that a section was cut, in 1947, through the Cursus as near as possible to the grave; this yielded another fragment of bluestone, this time of Cosheston sandstone, from the ditch. Intensive search of the ground in the neighbourhood resulted in the discovery of numerous chippings representing most of the known varieties of rocks at Stonehenge, but none in the intervening fields separating the two sites. This fact implies that a bluestone structure incorporating many Pembrokeshire varieties of stone *may* at some stage have existed near the west end of the Cursus, to be demolished and used later in the construction of the main monument.

The date of the erection of the main sarsen structure is now no longer a matter of mere speculation. The absence of contemporary domestic refuse and graves on so sacred a site is not to be wondered at, and this very fact has in the past raised numerous difficulties when efforts were made to interpret its age and history, and has been the cause of much argument. But, until recently, our only course has been to rely on certain external features, on the contents in fact of the many graves that surround the monument as does a cemetery its parish church, even though such an assumption lacked precision. To be precise one needed some internal feature, something actually attached to or forming part of the stones themselves. By great good fortune this was forthcoming in 1953, during an intensive photographic survey by R. J. C. Atkinson, in the form of a number of weather-beaten carvings on some of the stones, apparently contemporary with their original dressing, which until then had remained unobserved and unrecognized in spite of past observation and photographic zeal.

Plate 33

Stone 53 of the second trilithon was then found to have on its inner side at eye-level representations of bronze axe-blades and of a bronze dagger; these were subsequently confirmed by the discovery of other axe carvings on the outsides of the uprights of the outer circle, especially on those of stones 3 and 4. The forms here so clearly portrayed full size, belong to well-known types of flat and hammer-flanged axes with widely splayed cutting edges that were in current use during the Early Bronze Age and which were probably being manufactured in, and exported from, Ireland around 1500 B.C., though the type, especially those with cast flanges, was fundamentally of Central European origin. Very special interest may be attached, therefore, to such a decorated hammer-flanged specimen that was actually found within 500 yards of Stonehenge during pipe-laying operations in 1952. The significance of these axe carvings on the sacred stones can hardly be dissociated from the widespread axe-cult of Mediterranean origin which we have noticed had already been transmitted in modified form to the stone axes of the North by way of the Breton megalithic tombs.

Fig. 16

The carving of the hafted dagger with its long tapering blade and slight projecting shoulders at its base is even more informative. Since the axe carvings can be recognized as accurate copies of current types, we are entitled to assume that that of the dagger must be other than purely imaginative. Such a type is, however, unknown in north-western Europe during the Bronze Age when it would have been a simple matter to copy local native forms. Only one other carving seemingly portraying a similar type of dagger together with axes has been recorded and this comes from a grave slab of an early Bronze Age burial near Badbury Rings in Dorset. What, then, does the dagger represent? And does it provide the clue to the building of Stonehenge III we have awaited so long? Plate 34

The writer is of the opinion that it does for the reason that the nearest parallels come from the Culture of the Shaft Graves of Mycenæ, in which a type of dagger having much the same outline as the Stonehenge carving was in use from about 1600 to 1500 B.C. Now, this would imply that some trader or other from the Greek Mainland who was familiar with such weapons had visited Britain about this time, and that it may have been under his influence and inspiration that the building was erected, the carving representing, as it were, his signature or that of a mission, on completion. Such a sophisticated structure was clearly beyond the realms of the natives' imagination, although in design and proportion it could well have represented, so far from home, a pale reflection of Ægean architecture and masonry. In our next chapter we shall be considering some of the distant trade contacts of the Wessex Culture that embraced both Continental Europe and the Mycenæan world. It is gradually becoming more and more apparent that the idea of expeditions from the Ægean to the barbarian North, and even possibly the establishment of trading posts in Wessex, is not so far-fetched as they might at first appear. As we shall see, the legendary voyages of the Argo in search of the Golden Fleece may not merely be old wives' tales, but could conceivably enshrine vague folk memories of early expeditions in search of gold, copper and amber.

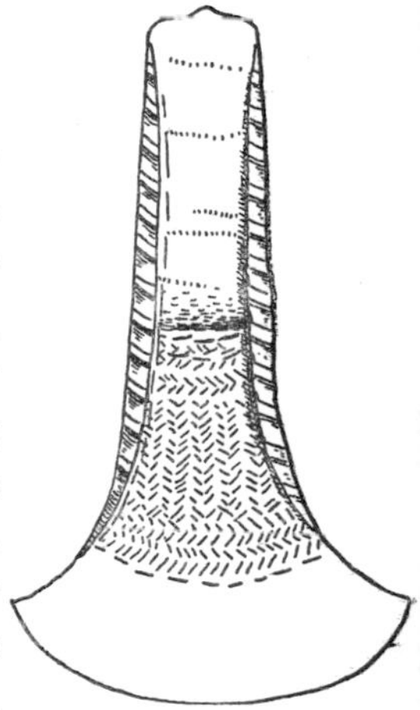

Fig. 16 Decorated bronze axe-blade, found near Stonehenge. Length 4¼ in.

STONEHENGE IIIB

The next building phase appears to have been concerned with attempts to blend and incorporate *some* of the bluestones now *Fig. 17* lying idle from the dismantled and unfinished period II structure. This is certainly the most difficult phase to interpret, since it was clearly a period of indecision and seems to have formed no part of the originally conceived plan. Apparently the first intention was to erect a double bluestone circle outside the lintelled sarsen circle in the fifty-nine 'Z' and 'Y' holes, in a manner that was both geometrically and æsthetically most unsatisfactory. The holes for these circles were certainly dug, but excavation has proved that they never actually held stones or had ever been refilled. All contained an accumulation of air-borne soil with various objects, including bluestone chippings, disposed throughout in positions consistent with the subsequent action of earthworms. For some reason this project was abandoned, perhaps through a human or natural catastrophe.

The problem of greatest complexity, however, involves the shape and contents of the small internal bluestone structure within the central space enclosed by the five trilithons, which
Plate 35 was in the last phase to contain the present bluestone horseshoe. We know that this last IIIC phase contained dressed bluestones from an earlier structure including two very shapely lintels worked in the very best style and clearly tooled to shape and dressed under the eye of the original architect; and we know
Plate 36 also that these lintels had rested for a time on uprights, as patches of polish imparted through thermal expansion and contraction at the point of contact of upright and lintel are unmistakably present on one. But we do not know conclusively that these lintels actually formed part of this earlier IIIB structure in view of the possibility of the presence of another bluestone structure at the west end of the Cursus.

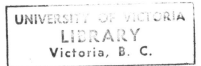

Plate 31 However, excavations in 1954 and 1956 yielded the valuable information that an oval or elliptical setting of stone-holes had originally held stone uprights and had formerly stood within this central area. These had been filled in with compacted chalk rubble which in one instance had at a later date been dug

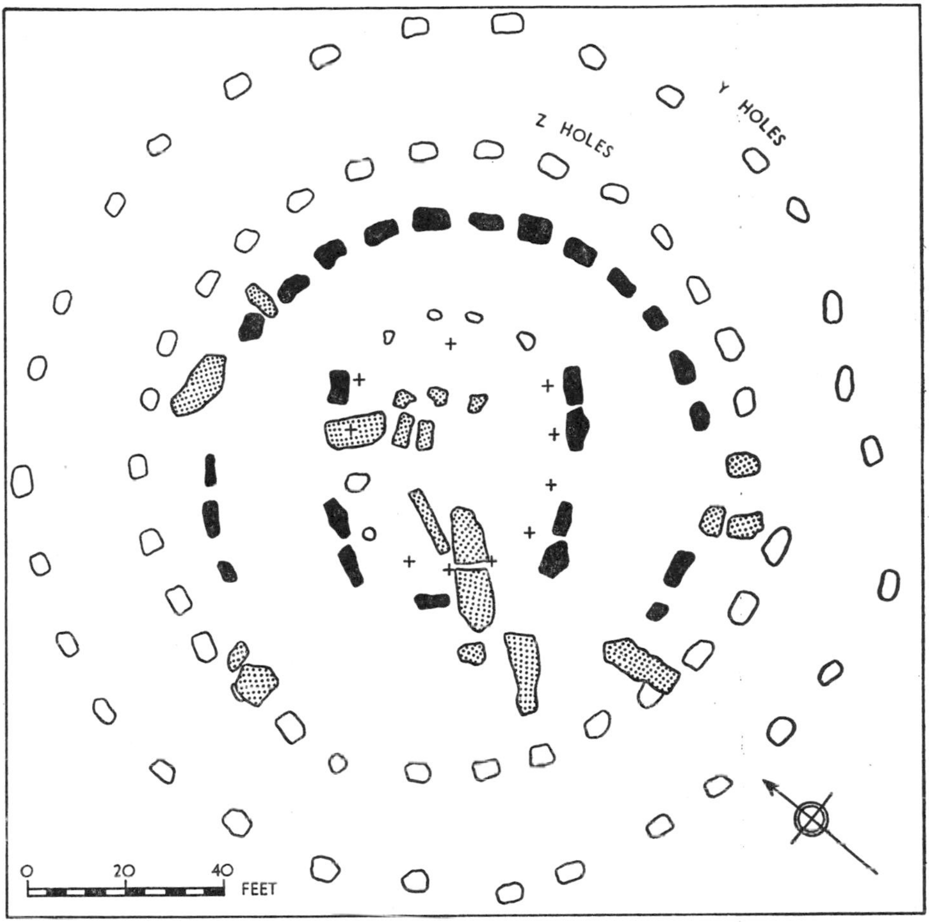

Fig. 17 Plan of Stonehenge in Phase IIIb. Standing sarsens black, fallen sarsens stippled, stone-holes for bluestones in outline, suggested positions marked by crosses

into for the purpose of erecting an upright of the last IIIC phase; but in so doing the end of the stone had been accidentally broken off and had therefore to be used as a chock stone to raise the monolith to the required height. But even more surprisingly, this particular filled-in IIIB stone-hole was found to have been dug into the filling of an even earlier trench or elongated stone-hole that had two clearly defined stone impressions on its base. Here we may well have evidence of some internal bluestone setting contemporary with the period II unfinished double circles; but future excavations alone can disentangle the details of this implied and complex sequence.

STONEHENGE IIIC

Fig. 10; Plates 26, 29, 35

The last and final phase of reconstruction is, as might be expected, the clearest, though the manner in which the bluestones were re-used does not suggest the hand of a master-builder. It could well, in fact, have taken place a century or so after the completion of the original sarsen masterpiece, i.e., round about 1400 B.C.

The decision to remodel the bluestone elements is likely to have followed fairly rapidly after the abandonment of the 'Z' and 'Y' hole plan; and it is evident that very special care was taken to efface as far as possible memories of the former bluestone structures. The two beautifully shaped lintels were now relegated to inferior positions as mere uprights, with their mortise holes turned outwards, along with the undressed boulders in the newly planned single circle inside the sarsen circle. Excavations have shown that the sixty-odd stones of this circle, mostly now robbed or intentionally battered to below ground level, were very closely set more or less on a circle lying midway between the old 'Q' and 'R' holes of the period II double circle and not infrequently resting on the chalk rubble filling of the dumb-bell-shaped holes connecting them.

The inner bluestone horseshoe also took shape at this time. Having dismantled the older oval setting and any other existing bluestone features, nineteen of the longest and most elegant were erected in the form of a horseshoe within the area of the sarsen trilithons. All those now existing are of spotted dolerite

Fig. 18 Isometric drawing of Stonehenge central area before re-erection of stones in 1958

or preselite, and all have been most carefully dressed to obelisk-like shape. Many are missing and a number are defaced, but amongst them are two of outstanding interest as they must have formed part of the earlier structure. One has a longitudinal groove down its length while the other, now buried below one of the fallen stones of the great trilithon, possesses a corresponding tongue. *Fig. 18*

The so-called Altar Stone of micaceous sandstone from the Milford Haven region lies recumbent below two of the fallen stones of the same trilithon. It is the largest bluestone at Stonehenge, being 16 feet long by 3½ feet wide and 1¾ feet thick, and has been dressed. At present nothing is known about its original setting or whether it now rests as originally intended.

We have no evidence for any reconstruction of the sarsen features of the monument and so must consider the building as being now complete and the venerated centre of a wide and important district. So far we have discussed its bare bones, but these bones were constructed by man; by men in fact who, in the later phases at least, seem to have been dissatisfied with the way in which their sacred bluestones had or had not been incorporated into the superlative sarsen design they so fully appreciated and unquestionably revered, but who were as yet undecided as to the final form the building should take. The master-builder was no longer with them to guide them, and so they had no other choice but to revert to their old traditional practice of erecting the bluestones as a plain uninspired monolithic horseshoe and circle within, and architecturally unconnected with, the sarsen structure.

It now remains for us to examine and infer what we can of the people likely to have been implicated in its construction, and the cause of its elevation towards the southern edge of Salisbury Plain.

Chapter IX

Heroes and Traders

THE MEASURE OF COHERENCE and cultural unity imposed by the Beaker and Single-Grave invaders of Northern Germany and the Rhine on the previous population of the British Isles, and their genius for exploration and exploitation, was now to reap its reward. Trade contacts had been established with Irish metallurgists who had awaited the necessary stimulus and urge to develop their industrial activities already implanted in Ireland from Iberia; and connections had been maintained with their Continental kith and kin who were no doubt kept appraised of western potentialities in supplies of copper, tin and gold. Here we need but recall the Irish gold discs from Mere and Monkton Farleigh which may even in their designs copy the decoration of the heads of racquet pins of Central European Early Bronze Age type and have been made at the behest of the Beaker-Folk. Plates 17, 18

The old transpeninsular waterways connecting the Bristol Channel with the English Channel and the Continent, which skirted the southern edge of Salisbury Plain, were now to see an ever-increasing flow of traffic. This traffic was to result in the temporary and almost fabulous enrichment of certain local members of the Secondary Neolithic society, chieftains or potential mercantile aristocrats fully prepared to enrich themselves, but unprepared and incapable of adding much to the sum of human endeavour other than by stimulating artisans and craftsmen and thus ushering in the brilliant Early Bronze Age that was destined to have so far-reaching an effect on Europe. The growth of Wessex was without question based on trade, but on a form of trade organized solely perhaps to satisfy the personal aggrandisement of a warrior aristocracy of 'heroic' outlook. It would seem that the pattern of human society was now to become a barbaric reflection of that embodied in the Homeric poems, with power concentrated in the hands of a chieftain class, a pattern that spread right across Europe with Mycenæ at its apex. In the words of Professor Hawkes, 'The pride of the chieftain demands costly finery and weapons of war and ceremonial, which will be interchanged as 'presents' even over great distances: this feature of Mycenaean culture is constantly portrayed in the Homeric poems, and when the archæologist speaks of such interchange as 'trade', he does well to remember it as a social as much as an economic phenomenon.'

Our knowledge of the period immediately following the establishment of Beaker and Single-Grave dominance is derived almost exclusively from the contents of graves under round barrows. No hiatus in the archæological record can be discerned, merely an increase in material wealth occasioned by expanding commercial connexions and the gradual fusion by intermarriage and absorption of the various cultural traits we have already noted. Unfortunately we have absolutely no knowledge whatsoever of the existence of any contemporary habitation or occupation site in Wessex. This is all the more surprising in areas of such high barrow density as those of Dorset and Wiltshire, and to a very great extent limits our understanding of the people themselves. Where and how they lived we just do not know; but there can be no doubt about their intense desire to furnish their dead with suitable and costly trappings for the underworld.

Round barrows constitute by far the most numerous group of prehistoric earthworks on the chalk and surrounding downs; in Wessex alone some six thousand have been recorded, and without doubt many more have been destroyed by the plough. Many have suffered considerably in the past from ransacking by treasure seekers and from explorations by former antiquaries of an earlier school whose techniques of excavation were necessarily primitive. However, we should be grateful to a few of them for their records and for preserving some of the objects discovered. In two sumptuous volumes entitled *Ancient Wiltshire,* Sir Richard Colt Hoare described and illustrated the contents of the many barrows which he and William Cunnington dug on Salisbury Plain in the early years of the nineteenth century; and somewhat later, Charles Warne did a similar service for the barrows of Dorset, but less satisfactorily.

It was not until 1938, however, that Professor Piggott analysed the contents of a number of these explored barrows and was able to show that many of distinctive type contained grave-goods which represented a consistent culture sharply demarcated from their predecessors and which included objects indicating very widespread European trade contacts. His distribution maps demonstrated that the main nucleus of the culture was centred in Wiltshire with the Stonehenge district at its nodal point, though outlying extensions of the culture occurred also in Dorset, Devon and Cornwall, eastwards sporadically to Sussex, and northwards to the Upper Thames Valley with related but smaller centres in Norfolk and eastern Yorkshire. Appropriately enough, he termed the culture the 'Wessex Culture' of the British Bronze Age, whilst fully appreciating the one-sided nature of the evidence derived from graves only. Certain types of pottery vessels, metal and other substances are virtually unknown outside Wiltshire, whilst their distribution and that of other articles clearly mark Salisbury Plain as the core of this Early British Bronze Age which now grew with such vigour and flourished through direct contacts with Ireland, Central Europe and the Mediterranean World.

The barrows themselves are of very varied form, though few have been excavated by modern standards. The Bowl-shaped ones are by far the most numerous, whilst those that have been proved by their contents to belong specifically to the Wessex

Plate 37

Culture are very distinctive in shape and have been known since Thurnam's day as Bell, Disc, Saucer and Pond barrows, all of which frequently occur together in closely knit groups. All but the last are characterized by having an encircling, usually continuous, ditch carefully and often accurately dug with a wide flat base, and hence can be grouped together as Circle Barrows. The so-called Pond barrow, about which we shall say more later, does not contain an internal mound, but consists of a pond-like circular area up to 100 feet in diameter with an embanked rim.

The burial rite was either by inhumation or cremation, and the associated grave-goods suggest that the former was the earlier in the case of male burials but that this was later superseded by the universal rite of cremation, a practice that we have seen was already in use in Late Neolithic times. This reassertion of the rite, after the first impact of the Beaker-Folk habit of inhumation had receded, may conceivably have been due to female influence, since there is some reason for thinking that a preference for cremation may have persisted throughout in the female line. At all events, it would seem that the rite of Disc barrow burial was reserved very largely for women-folk.

Unfortunately we know very little about contemporary burial ritual. In a few instances some form of mortuary-house can be inferred within the mound, whilst in others, dug-out coffins—possible boats to the underworld—were used. But not until more careful barrow excavations on the lines of those recently carried out by N. and C. Thomas on Snail Down, and P. Ashbee near Bulford, can we expect any great advance in knowledge of structural features or other rites accompanying the actual inhumation or cremation of the body.

Nowhere is the barrow concentration more marked than in

Fig. 9

the Stonehenge region. Here are to be seen cemeteries suggesting dynastic or tribal groupings of burials under barrows, with what we may call a 'Founder's Grave' containing a Beaker often associated and sometimes a long barrow as well. The impressive Winterbourne Stoke Cross-roads group is a particularly good instance of this and, although not so well documented, the Normanton group with the famous Bush Barrow as possibly its earliest member. Similar but smaller groups of Circle Barrows are to be seen in Dorset, especially on Oakley Down, in the Avebury district and elsewhere in Wiltshire. These barrow cemeteries with a 'Founder's Grave' attached are important as proving continuity of tradition from Beaker times well into those of the Wessex Culture, with cremation replacing inhumation as the sequence progresses. Primary burial in these cemeteries was probably accorded only to members of the ruling or wealthier classes; a considerable body of evidence exists for the presence of secondary interments of the less distinguished or poorer relations in these and earlier mounds, as for instance in the Stockbridge barrow already referred to with its small necklace of imported beads and bronze awl.

The contents of the graves are very varied, some being of indigenous origin, others clearly imports or close copies. Furthermore, it is now apparent that the culture can be divided into two phases, an earlier one centred round 1500 B.C. with its inhumation graves, grooved bronze daggers, probably amber space-plate necklaces and some of the cups of the Aldbourne Plates 38, 39, 55
and Manton types; and a later one around 1400 B.C. embracing cremations, sometimes in cinerary urns, incense or pygmy cups, Plates 58, 59
ogival bronze daggers and faience beads. However, in neither phase can any form of mass migration or invasion be inferred comparable with that of the earlier Beaker invasions. The obvious derivation of much from the parallel Bronze Age communities of Central Europe and especially of the Saale-Elbe region of Saxo-Thuringia, which was itself in close touch with the great Aunjetitz Culture of Bohemia, and the contemporary appearance of elements of a similar culture in

Brittany (the 'dagger graves') suggest westward movements of merchants or traders in quest of metals rather than of small bands of a conquering military aristocracy. For we must not forget that the Early Bronze Age of Saxo-Thuringia was also based on the same Single-Grave traditions as those of Wessex with similar richly furnished barrow burials and timber mortuary-houses, and that these regions must have remained closely linked both commercially and by kinship.

The native element is especially marked in the pottery forms and insignia of prestige. But here again we must never forget that we are dealing almost entirely with grave-goods. Vessels of beaker type suddenly cease to be deposited with the dead; but we do not know whether they continued in use for domestic purposes. Their place was taken initially by small cups of the Aldbourne and Manton types derived almost certainly from Rinyo-Clacton wares developed locally and in parallel from the same Chassey II source as the *vase-support* of Brittany and the Channel Islands; they were slightly later to emerge as the incense or pygmy cups accompanying cremations in the Middle Bronze Age. Some of the latter look remarkably like representations of Stonehenge itself. Larger vessels of tripartite collared form also begin to appear as food vessels with inhumations, and these again later develop into the normal and universal receptacles for cremations. We now know that these collared urns were also derived from local Secondary Neolithic wares, since early specimens have been found with other Late Neolithic pots in the West Kennet long barrow. Here they had been used in the first place for domestic purposes, an aspect we know so little about, and it was only later that they were deemed worthy to accompany the dead. We cannot disregard the fact that these substitutes for the sepulchral beaker may imply the rise to power of a new dominant caste having a considerable Secondary Neolithic background, the Beaker element meanwhile having become absorbed or submerged.

Plates 38, 39

Plate 40

However, two or three vessels suggest imports from farther afield. A small undecorated cup with handle from Collingbourne Ducis closely resembles the large series of handled vessels of the Central European Bronze Age, whilst a similar one with four small feet from Oakley Down represents a well-known Aunjetitz type.

We have already noted the native burial from Upton Lovel with its bone-fringed garment, stone tools and battle-axes, and *Fig. 13* other objects that formally belong to the Wessex Culture. To a similar native origin we must also ascribe the ceremonial sceptres or maces of authority. The Bush Barrow mace, of Plates 41, 42 attractive fossiliferous limestone probably from the Teignmouth district, with its zigzag bone inlays is a famous example and with it should be included the even more ornate gold-studded shale specimen from the Clandon Barrow near Dorchester found with an amber cup, a lozenge-shaped gold Plates 43, 44 plate and a bronze dagger. Well made and sometimes ornamented stone battle-axes with symmetrically expanded blade Plate 13 and butt fall into the same class of native object developed possibly to resemble the profile of the Minoan double-axe, four bronze examples of which have been found in the British Isles. Some of these stone battle-axes are now known to have emanated from picrite outcrops at Cwm Mawr near Corndon in Shropshire, others from the Whin Sill of the Teesdale area. Grooved arrow-straighteners, whetstones, bone tweezers and flint and pyrites for making fire often accompany the dead; whilst from one of the Normanton barrows a perforated swan's bone has been interpreted as a musical pipe.

But it is only when we examine the remarkable increase in armament that we begin to appreciate to the full the emergence of the true Bronze Age with its repertory of bronze daggers, Plates 47–50 spear-heads, knives, axes, awls and tracers. All have been Plate 46 found in Wessex Culture graves; spear-heads occur only in quantity in the two well-known trader's hoards from Arreton

Down and Totland, both in the Isle of Wight. The bronzes themselves appeared initially through trade relations with Central Europe, but were soon copied and often improved by smiths in the British Isles, whose introduction of the bronze halberd was to be so eagerly accepted in return. Wessex itself, through lack of raw materials, never became an industrial centre for bronze manufacture; its unique position attracted products from elsewhere but it never seems to have acted other than as an *entrepôt* for their dissemination over wider fields. Nevertheless, the right situation had been created and the impetus given for the British Isles now to enter the forefront of the newly awakened bronze industry.

The daggers characteristic of the period are of two main (Plate 41) types. The earlier forms, as those from Bush Barrow, are often large with grooves parallel to the blade and with six rivets for fixing to the haft; they are closely related to both Breton and Saxo-Thuringian types. The later forms are ogival in shape with grooves, a thickened midrib and normally three rivets at the heel. They also may be of Central European origin, or (Plates 47–50) represent parallel developments in the British Isles. But the hafts and pommels are on occasion characteristically British and were possibly developed from specimens of the Milston type. Some of these hafts are richly decorated with thousands of tiny gold pins arranged in zones and zigzags; whilst the pommels (of Central European types) may be of bone or (Plate 45) amber, again ornamented with gold pins or plating. This gold pin technique was, however, in current use by Mycenæan armourers, and for the original inspiration we may have perhaps to turn our eyes in that direction.

(Plates 41, 46; *Fig. 16*) Bronze axe-blades of hammer-flanged type are almost certainly of Irish origin, but cast-flanged axes of similar type were being imported into our eastern counties from Germany. Crutch-headed, ring-headed and globe-headed pins were now in normal use in Central Europe for fastening clothing, but not in this country where as we have seen, V-perforated buttons, now sometimes gold-plated, were in vogue; the occasional appearance of these pins in Wessex Culture contexts may be presumed to denote trade relations; but they do not seem to have found much favour.

Gold was certainly being imported from Ireland, but probably in the raw state for working up into ornaments by local Plates 42, 43, 44, 45 craftsmen, as the objects produced are not found in that country. Extensive use was made of the metal mainly in the form of decorated thin sheets for attachment to wood, leather or conical shale buttons, and also for beads and pendants. Two Plates 56, 57 of the finest gold plates came from Bush Barrow and from Clandon Barrow in Dorset, the former also with a magnificent gold-plated belt-hook of Central European type. The truly astonishing ribbed gold cup from Rillaton in Cornwall, with its close Mycenæan parallels in gold-working technique, Plate 52 might almost represent a Mycenæan gift to some contemporary British chieftain.

Amber, that much prized golden fossil resin of the Ancient World, still deemed of value, looms large in the products of the North that found their way to the Mediterranean. As we might expect, the Wessex barrows contain numerous objects of the material mainly in the shape of beads and pendants. Plates 54, 55, 57, 60 Small quantities may have been obtained from our eastern coasts but these could never have been adequate to meet all demands. A large piece of raw amber weighing 2¾ oz., found at Westbury in Wiltshire in 1956, may have been so derived but unfortunately it is now impossible to know whether it was lost accidentally at the time. No doubt much was obtained direct from the Baltic, the home of European amber; the necklace of amber, segmented tin and segmented faience beads from Odoorn, Holland, and the segmented faience bead from Fjallerslev in Jutland support a direct northern coastal route to the mouth of the Elbe, as do also a number of Danish amber beads which copy in detail some of imported faience found in Wessex Culture contexts.

But fabricated amber ornaments were also arriving from other sources. Three small pendants representing hafted Plates 54, 57 halberds found at Hengistbury Head (the main port to Wessex), at Normanton and Manton must have been inspired by the parade weapons of Central Europe. Each of these miniature objects, perforated for suspension, has a small bronze blade held in a shaft in two instances, of amber, and in two instances bound with gold wire or plate; they must symbolize in trinket form the typical metal-shafted halberds of Saxo-Thuringia. Also to be considered are necklaces of a distinctive type possessing complex transversely perforated spacing-plates to Plate 55 separate multiple strings of beads. This particular form of spacing-plate is not known in northern Europe but appears in south-western Germany around the headwaters of the Rhine and the Danube, and even more significantly in early Mycenæan tombs, as at Kakovatos, *c.* 1450 B.C., clearly proving amongst other things that Mycenæan trade relations had been established along this European route to the British Isles and linked with the great amber route from the Baltic to Greece via the Brenner Pass and the Adriatic. Decorated gold-mounted Plates 54, 57 amber discs, possibly representing solar amulets, have been found at Normanton and Manton; these may well have been traded along the same route and, as pointed out by J. M. de Navarro, are more than likely to have emanated from the Ægean, since a similar one with plain gold band was found in the Tomb of the Double-Axes at Knossos, and closely related but more elaborate ones of steatite are known from Enkomi in Cyprus.

However, without question, two of the finest objects found in the Wessex Culture are handled cups carved from single pieces of amber. One perfect specimen of red amber, which Plate 51 can hold nearly half a pint, was found in a barrow at Hove with a battle-axe, of pronounced double-axe profile, and a bronze dagger; the other, now fragmentary, came from the famous Clandon Barrow in Dorset. Closely related cups of local shale are also known from Wiltshire and Farway Down, Devon. Plate 53

But nothing can stir the imagination more than the evidence that exists for direct contacts with the literate civilizations of the Mediterranean world at this time. We have noted the appearance of a few exotic objects which may very likely be of Ægean if not Mycenæan derivation, and to these we may add a stone axe of emery or corundum from Calne, Wiltshire, which almost certainly originated from Naxos or a nearby island of the Greek archipelago. Such objects, however, are not very numerous and could well have arrived in Britain in the normal course of trade through passage from hand to hand.

When we come to examine the dissemination of numerous small articles of jewellery in the form of cheap brightly coloured beads, the matter assumes a very different light. Here we are almost certainly dealing with the by-products of trade expeditions or missions to far-off lands where a handful or so of attractively coloured trinkets had already been found to appeal to primitive minds, and which were valued in proportion to their relative scarcity. The remarkable synthetic material of which these beads were made is known as 'ancient faience' and appears to have been invented and later developed only by oriental communities that had reached a relatively high level of civilization. The industry, which involved a high degree of technological specialization and which was later to develop into the great glass industry of modern times, was in fact confined to the manufacture of such luxury articles and personal ornaments as beads, amulets, statuettes, seals and small vases that were required mainly to satisfy æsthetic needs, and could not be expected to enter into the economic life of more primitive peoples existing at lower levels of civilization. The evidence we possess at present suggests that faience was first invented in northern Mesopotamia during the fifth millennium B.C. and that it was only later introduced into Egypt in Predynastic times, where it found a congenial home and blossomed from then onwards into one of major importance for some three thousand years at least. Although in course of time the industry spread to the neighbouring civilizations of the Ægean and the Indus, it never appears to have attained in those regions the immense popularity that we find it did throughout all periods of Dynastic Egypt.

Faience is not a natural product but consists of a composite material formed by glazing a moulded core of finely powdered quartz grains already thermally fused together by the addition of small amounts of an alkali or lime, or both. The subsequent act of glazing involved the application of a pre-made soda-lime-quartz glass in powdered form as a slip to the pre-moulded core, the glass itself having usually been coloured bright turquoise blue or green by the addition during fusion of traces of copper compounds. An alternative and simpler process consisted in the use of powdered coloured glass alone to bind the quartz grains together; this process, after firing, resulted in a coloured matrix, the whole object being coloured uniformly throughout with the quartz grains appearing to float in a lake of glass. It will be appreciated that in both processes a preformed coloured glass had first to be made; nevertheless, this was not used as such for many centuries, the powdered material being used solely as a slip for the external glazing of moulded quartz cores.

It was not, however, until the second half of the second millennium B.C. that Egypt witnessed a sudden expansion of its glass and faience industries with a prodigious increase in the volume of goods turned out for both home consumption and foreign trade. During the XVIIIth Dynasty (1580-1314 B.C.) especially, factories such as those at Tell-el-Amarna were working at high pressure—they have been found littered with waste products and thousands of pottery moulds for making beads and pendants. Syria and Mycenæan Greece did not lag behind but their output never approached that of Egypt. Until the XVIIIth Dynasty the products of such factories had been confined to relatively restricted areas of the Middle East, to those areas in fact in which the four major literate civilizations had their being. But from 1500 B.C. onwards the new element of distant trade expeditions suddenly makes its appearance, and this almost certainly may be connected with the rise to power of the Greek Mainlanders with their wide sea-borne commercial interests and insatiable desire for precious and base metals, amber and other exotic substances.

We now encounter faience and glass beads of Eastern Mediterranean derivation scattered as trade beads along well defined routes and over vast distances; around the Black Sea to the Caucasus and the shores of the Caspian, and even up the Volga and Ural Rivers to Siberia; up the Nile to Central East Africa; up the Danube to Hungary, Poland and Moravia; and along the Mediterranean to the South of France and thence to the British Isles and the North. But these routes are almost precisely those hypothetically ascribed in ancient times to the legendary expeditions of Jason and the Argo in their quest for gold. Though it is highly speculative, the present writer feels that we can detect in the general scatter of these beads concrete echoes of these ancient Greek legends of commercial enterprise and exploratory voyages.

Certainly by 1450-1300 B.C. the Mycenæan commercial system embraced considerable areas of the Mediterranean, and faience beads appear in quantity in Malta, Sicily, the Lipari Islands and the South of France. From here they have been traced, together with small wire-wound glass beads, down the Garonne to the Atlantic coasts where they appear again in Brittany and in the British Isles.

Three distinct varieties amongst others are recognized in the British Isles: the segmented, the star and the quoit beads. The segmented variety is by far the most numerous, and the beads are concentrated mainly in the centre of the Wessex Culture where no less than thirty-three groups have been recorded from barrow burials. This particular form of bead was for long a favourite in Egypt, though beads of the exact shape and size of those found in Wessex appear only during a restricted period of the XVIIIth Dynasty. Identical beads have been found on a necklace from a grave at Abydos with a scarab of Amenhotep III (1408-1372 B.C.), and on another from Lachish in Palestine associated with a plaque of Amenhotep II (1450-1425 B.C.). It is thus possible to date with a fair degree of accuracy the appearance of these beads in graves of the Wessex Culture to between 1400 and 1300 B.C.

Fig. 19; Plate 60

Strangely enough the star and quoit beads, though in general contemporary with the segmented variety, lie peripherally to Wessex and are found mainly in graves nearer the coastline. This remarkable distribution could conceivably be due to a second expedition aimed not primarily at the heart of Wessex but largely coastally to spy out the lie of the land. It is remarkable, too, that the only analogues of these beads in Europe appear from a pile-dwelling on Lake Constance, from just that area from which our amber spacing beads with their Mycenæan connections were most probably derived. On the other hand, a small four-rayed faience star bead, typical of those found with segmented beads in Hungary and in Greece, has recently been discovered by G. V. Taylor in a cremation cemetery at Stainsby in Lincolnshire. This can only have arrived in the course of trade from the Middle Danube and very strongly supports the view that all British faience beads are of Eastern Mediterranean derivation.

Unfortunately it has so far proved impossible to deduce with accuracy the exact country of origin of many of these faience

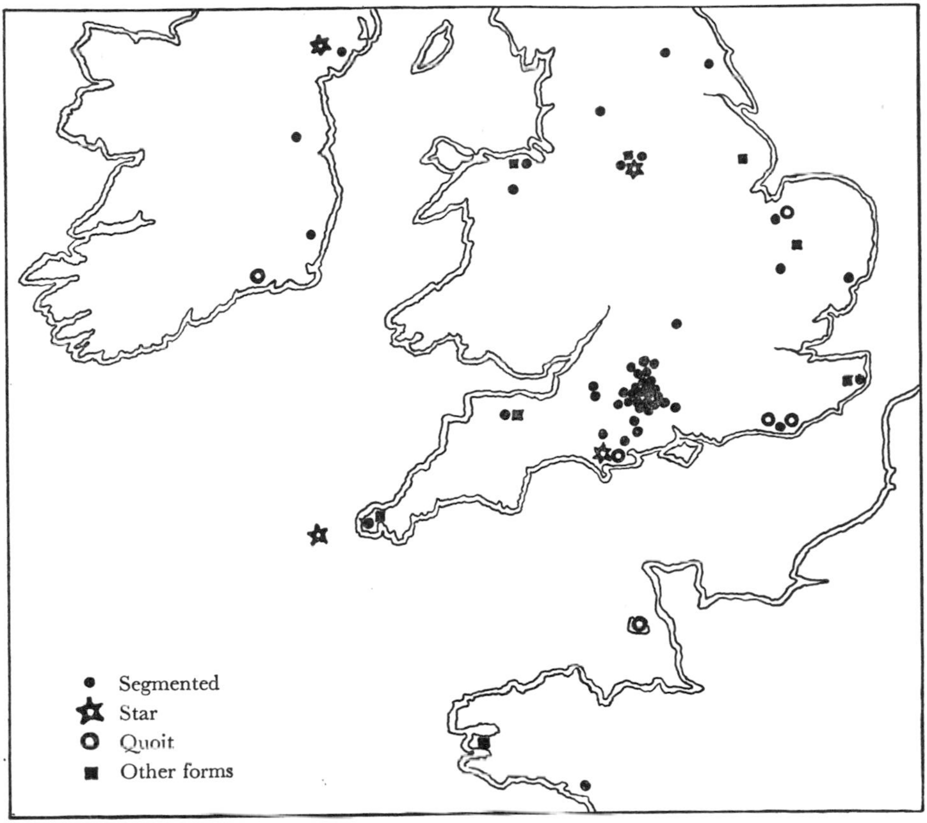

Fig. 19 Distribution of faience beads in part of the British Isles and France

beads. Spectrographic analysis has given equivocal results and we are, therefore, still forced to rely on morphological characters and archæological associations; but the present writer would nevertheless hazard the guess that great numbers of these trade beads will eventually be found to have emanated from Egyptian workshops even though disseminated by other seafaring people of Mediterranean origin.

If, then, we review in rapid summary the information we have been able to glean from the contents of the Wessex Culture tombs that surround Stonehenge, we find that we are presented with a consistent picture of dynastic or tribal groupings of burials of a rich aristocratic community that flourished between *c.* 1550 and 1300 B.C. The cause of its rise to power and wealth was due to its position on an exceedingly important trade route between the metalliferous regions of the West, and the Continent; but, as we shall see, when that trade stopped through the discovery and exploitation of metal deposits elsewhere, Wessex rapidly declined and entered a phase of almost complete stagnation. But during its *floruit,* it is by no means improbable that trading posts ultimately of Mycenæan origin may have been established possibly somewhere on the Wiltshire Avon near Amesbury; and we may even be rash enough to infer that their presence was the direct cause of the building of Stonehenge IIIA about 1500 B.C., at which time sufficient cultural cohesion had been secured to warrant such an outstanding achievement, never again to be repeated.

CHAPTER X

Aftermath

FROM ABOUT 1300 B.C. ONWARDS the rich Wessex Culture ceases to be perceptible as an archæological entity. Founded, as we have seen, exclusively on trade and on its fortunate position on a most important trade route, the culture may be considered as almost a parasitic growth that was bound to collapse when its life-blood was diverted to other quarters. The culture appears as the expression of an heroic aristocracy amassing unproductive weapons and luxury articles, and doubtless supported by an agricultural society. Nevertheless, under the favourable conditions created, the population may well have increased and have moved to new regions beyond Wessex. We have evidence of the widespread practice of cremation, with the ashes frequently contained in a pottery jar or cinerary urn, over the whole of the British Isles, to Caithness and Ireland and even oversea to Holland; archæology only gives us glimpses of a culture characterized by these cremated burials in large cinerary urns of varied form and decoration often accompanied by small pygmy vessels but usually, in the South, without other grave-goods. These cinerary urns are usually of the so-called 'collared' variety, but it is now recognized, as demonstrated by J. J. Butler and I. F. Smith, that other forms, such as the biconical type with horseshoe, and other finger-tipped, applied decoration, were also currently in use. These, until recently, have been attributed to the Late Bronze Age Deverel-Rimbury Culture, but it now seems clear that they too were derived from native Secondary Neolithic wares. Wessex no longer affords us evidence of an heroic warrior aristocracy, owing to the changing traditions of funerary ritual, but we need not assume that the region necessarily became a cultural backwater, a dismal and dreary period

Plates 61–63

unlit by any spark of human endeavour. Developments in bronze technology at this time, for instance, are discussed below.

The collapse of the Wessex Culture might be correlated, as Professor Childe has suggested, with the large-scale exploitation by deep mining of the copper lodes of the Eastern Alps probably under Mycenæan influence. The Mycenæan World needed ever-increasing supplies of bronze, and no other rich civilization of the period could afford to subsidize the required specialist labour and at the same time consume the product. The resultant abundance and cheapness of bronze that now flooded the markets of Europe gradually diverted Ægean interest from the British Isles, and was the direct cause of the subsequent rise of the Late Bronze Age on the Continent which followed the slow decline and exhaustion of the brilliant Mycenæan Empire soon after 1250 B.C.

But the effect of these new sources of metal on the British Isles was not yet immediately apparent. The Irish-British bronze industries continued to expand locally and to maintain trade contacts with northern Europe. We now find as characteristic of the period, and largely as a result of contacts with northern Europe, the development and manufacture of bronze rapiers, palstaves (developed flanged axes with stop-ridges) and spearheads with sockets for firmer attachment to the shaft. Other bronze articles seem to have been confined mostly to metal-workers' tools and equipment; bronze was not yet abundant enough for ordinary daily use. The metal-workers themselves apparently formed a class apart and, as Professor Childe has emphasized, could be regarded almost as a separate society liberated from the bonds of local custom and able to enjoy freedom of movement and travel wherever they found markets for their products and skill. Their products are certainly very rarely found in graves; mostly they appear singly as lost objects or hidden in merchant's or trader's hoards, as did the twelve palstaves found in a gravel pit at Shappen near Burley in the New Forest. But such hoards and single bronzes are relatively rare in Wessex itself, though they become commoner as we penetrate westward into Somerset.

No Middle Bronze Age settlement sites have yet been identified; there may have been an increased element of pastoralism side-by-side with continued grain-growing and hunting. An oval enclosure 400 by 270 feet on Rams Hill in Berkshire (the only one of its kind) has been interpreted as a cattle enclosure of the period. Excavations proved the presence of one entrance with post-holes, the ditch being flat-bottomed and almost vertical-sided in the manner traditional since Neolithic times. Numerous sherds of a Middle Bronze Age collared urn, almost certainly domestic rather than sepulchral, were found scattered in a loamy layer in immediate contact with the primary silting at an early stage in the history of the ditch.

A possible pitfall trap for the capture of animals was discovered in 1938 on Stockbridge Down in Hampshire. The oval-shaped pit was found on excavation to measure 14 by 6 feet at the surface and to be 8 feet 6 inches deep with almost vertical sides. So steep were they that a terrier fell in during operations and had to be rescued. The greater part of the pit was filled with dirty chalk dust and rubble; superimposed on this were 18 inches of a Middle Bronze Age refuse layer sealed in by a further 18 inches of top soil. This Bronze Age layer contained numerous fragments of collared urns ornamented with twisted cord, calcined flints, animal teeth and bones—some burnt and some split longitudinally for extraction of the marrow, fragments of charcoal, a small bone awl and a fragment of a sandstone quern or rubber for grinding corn. Eleven flint scrapers, still formed by pressure flaking, were also recovered, which proved that flint was still in use for domestic purposes.

Two forms of contemporary native burial having certain ritual features in common, and rooted deeply in Secondary

Neolithic practices, have yet to be mentioned; the Pond barrows and the flat cremation cemeteries. The former were certainly in process of development during the period of the Wessex Culture, though their direct connection with that culture may ultimately be proved to be illusory. On the other hand, we have only two examples of recognized cremation cemeteries in Wessex. Although, as we shall see, one contained some poor Wessex Culture grave-goods, such cemeteries are a common feature of the Middle Bronze Age in the Highland Zone of Great Britain.

Pond barrows are circular depressions averaging 60 feet in diameter and delimited by an accurately constructed embanked rim. A few occur in the Avebury district but most of them are concentrated around Stonehenge and in Dorset amongst the extensive barrow-fields near Winterbourne Abbas. Their frequent association with Bell and Disc barrows has suggested that they were in some way connected with the Wessex Culture, but the few that were partly examined during the eighteenth and nineteenth centuries yielded so little that their date and purpose have remained open to question. Recently, however *Fig. 20* an example, on Sheep Down, Winterbourne Steepleton, in Dorset, has been most carefully excavated with surprising and interesting results. Here the whole of the inner area, about 2 feet below the surrounding chalk, had been paved with tightly packed flint nodules about 7 inches thick, below which, and just outside the edge, were thirty-four pits cut into the natural chalk. Of these, eight contained soil only, seven contained urnless cremations, whilst twenty contained pots mostly crushed, three with cremations and two with dismembered inhumations. Since only eleven of the pits had human remains in them, the excavators concluded that this Pond barrow was not primarily sepulchral but had been used as a place for offerings and other ritual purposes comparable with those of some of the henge monuments, and that its situation in close proximity to round

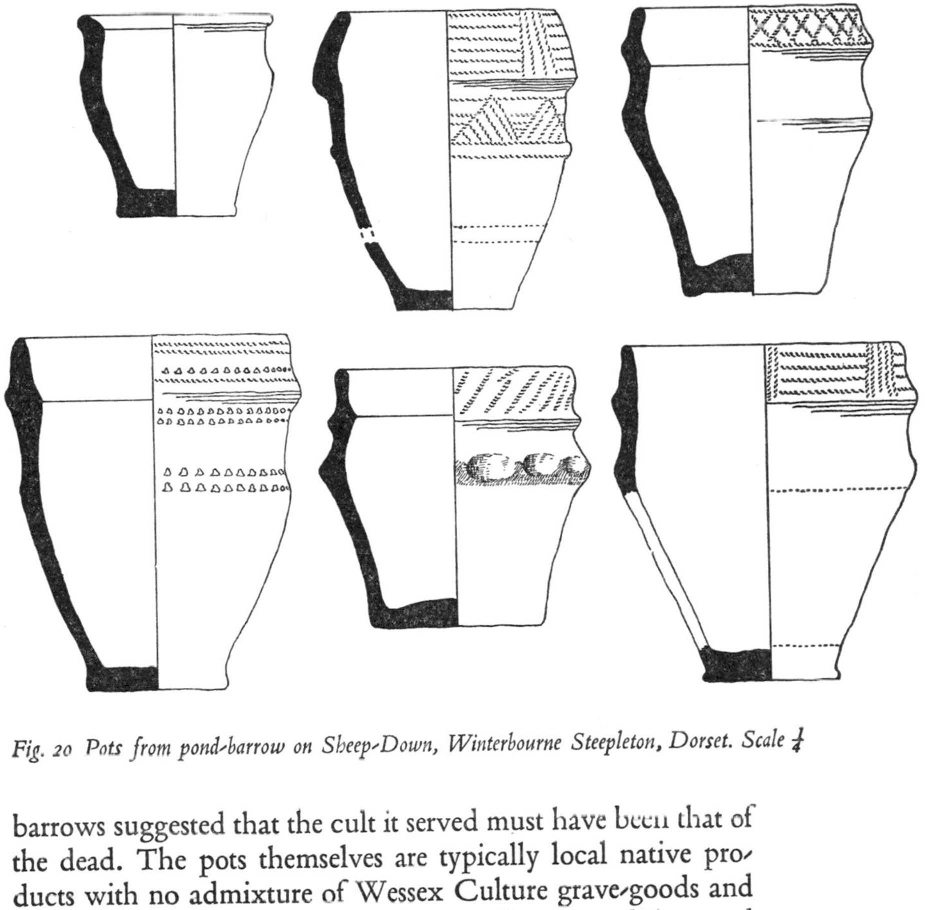

Fig. 20 Pots from pond-barrow on Sheep-Down, Winterbourne Steepleton, Dorset. Scale ¼

barrows suggested that the cult it served must have been that of the dead. The pots themselves are typically local native products with no admixture of Wessex Culture grave-goods and clearly imply the existence or persistence of native traditions and practices behind the Wessex Culture façade.

As long ago as 1866, C. Warne perceived the close relationship that must have existed between these Pond barrows and flat cremation cemeteries, when describing one of the latter found by agricultural labourers on Launceston Down in Dorset.

At a depth of 6 inches below the surface the workmen here found a compact bed of flints under which was much dark mould with charcoal, ashes, pieces of bone and potsherds; and cut into the chalk were numerous cists filled with cremations and ashes. A similar cemetery was found very much later by the present writer close to the flint-mine shafts on Easton Down. An area 60 feet by 20 feet, rising about 3 inches above the surrounding ground and undisturbed by rabbits, was also found to consist of a 6-inch layer of flint nodules and flint-mine debris including roughed-out axes. This layer covered seven small cists cut in the chalk, four of which contained urns, two urnless cremations, and one filled with mould only. The largest of the urns contained the cremated bones of an eight-year-old girl together with a small necklace of lignite and amber beads with one faience segmented bead and a small bone awl. Although these beads suggest a Wessex Culture date, they could as easily represent an heirloom buried a hundred or so years after the cessation of that culture. In any event, the presence of this native cemetery in the flint-mine area in such close proximity to the shafts and workshop floors can only imply that flint was still a useful commodity and that the mines were still being worked at this late stage, as seems to have been the case in the mines at Blackpatch in Sussex.

Fig. 21

The preservation of organic remains in the damp alkaline soils of the chalk-lands we should expect to be an exceedingly rare occurrence. For that very reason we cannot forbear from mentioning one very interesting secondary burial in an inverted urn of handled Cornish appearance found in 1814 in the famous 'Bell-Barrow of Chalk' at Winterslow near Salisbury. Here the conditions for preservation were favourable, the cremation within the urn appearing to have been wrapped in linen which had the appearance of fine lace and which blew away on exposure to the wind. Amongst the bones were a fluted bronze razor, now recognized as a Middle Bronze Age

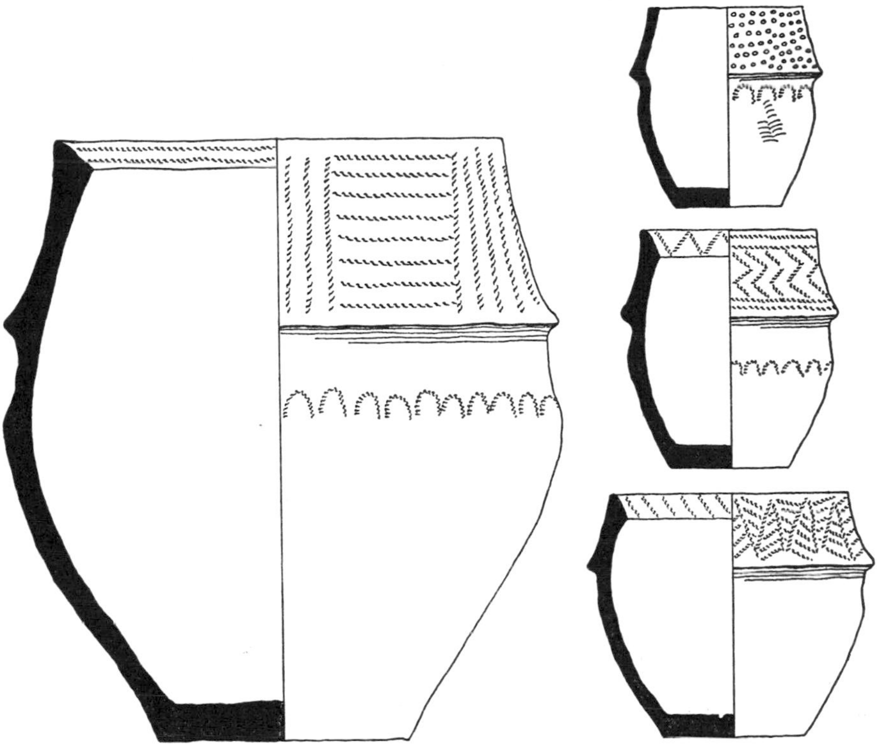

Fig. 21 Pots from the Easton Down cremation cemetery, Wilts. Scale ¼

type, a bronze awl, a necklace of amber beads, V-bored buttons and some human hair. Very fortunately this hair was preserved and now lies in the Ashmolean Museum at Oxford. Recent examination by J. L. Stoves has shown that it consists of human eyebrows from a number of individuals, which is an interesting sidelight on a contemporary mourning practice that has persisted to the present day amongst certain peoples.

CHAPTER XI

New Farmers

THE HAZE AND MIST that surrounds the 'heroic' stage of the Bronze Age past, its immediate aftermath now clears a little and we find ourselves no longer compelled to construct our picture of later prehistoric events in Wessex solely from the evidence available from burials, with their implications of chieftains and their followers whose burial rites involved the building of complex barrows and the decking of the dead with objects of prestige and adornment for display in an underworld. From 1000 B.C. onwards, thanks to archæological evidence from settlements as well as graves, we enter a world of a familiar if primitive pattern, and one which we can perhaps more easily understand. Thanks to the more abundant evidence and its nature, we can for the first time visualize men and women pursuing their daily tasks in a manner not dissimilar from that perceptible for instance in early medieval societies. In central and northern Europe from the twelfth century B.C. onwards there was a period of unrest and of technological development, not unconnected, it seems, with the break-up of the political balance of power in the Near East to be followed shortly by the emergence of Celtic-speaking and iron-using peoples. The Late Bronze and Early Iron Ages being periods of some complexity in Wessex, we can attempt only a bare outline here.

The relative abundance of bronze tools and their availability was now to place these commodities within the reach of a larger section of the population than in earlier times, whilst the introduction of new agricultural techniques presumably resulted in an increase in the food supply, allowing for a concomitant growth of population.

A new series of migrations to our southern shores is now perceptible in the archæological record, and may be attributed to the disturbed conditions on the European continent already mentioned. There resulted a displacement of groups of people including those of the retarded Tumulus Bronze Culture of the Middle Rhine and northern France. Some apparently migrated or were pushed farther west; others crossed the Channel. Amongst the first refugees from Picardy, Professor Hawkes has recognized certain settlers at Ramsgate in Kent and the Thames estuary, whilst others from the Seine-Somme region crossed to Sussex, where at sites such as Plumpton Plain we encounter evidence for new methods of agriculture: enclosed farmsteads associated with cattle-ways separating small, squarish fields, presumably cultivated with a traction-plough rather than with a hoe. This type of agricultural economy was to form the foundation of that which persisted in southern England up to, and into, the Roman occupation.

In Wessex, as elsewhere, we meet with the sporadic beginnings of a new and concurrent phenomenon, the appearance of hoards of bronze implements and ornaments buried or lost, perhaps an indication of a time of insecurity. These hoards, which appear in Britain in much greater numbers than those of earlier days, probably represent in some instances the stock-in-trade of itinerant smiths or tinkers, 'international' in all probability; and their contents throw a flood of light on the advances in metallurgical techniques that were now taking place on the Continent, and on the new types of tool and weapon that were now deemed common necessities. New types of tools and weapons of Continental origin, such as socketed axes, carpenter's tools including saws, gouges and chisels, and leaf-shaped swords capable of slashing as well as thrusting, were being peddled and copied, and the tinker was not averse to accepting in exchange broken and scrap metal for re-casting. Objects in beaten bronze, showing a knowledge of the technique of annealing, also appear in Britain for the first time.

But, as we have seen, Wessex had never been a centre of

bronze-working, due to the absence of raw materials. It seems also to have had little to offer in trade exchange for imported metal goods. But bronze hoards and single objects are widely distributed, mostly peripherally to the chalk massif along the south coast and in Somerset, with relatively few inland; the majority can be ascribed to the period of the migrations to Wessex under discussion, beginning probably about 1000 B.C. But before we glance at the contents of these hoards and at the wealth of articles that were now becoming available we should first meet the new immigrants themselves, named (not very happily) after their two well-known cemeteries in the Deverel barrow and at Rimbury in Dorset.

We have seen that owing to a variety of causes the period from the twelfth century B.C. onwards was one of disruption and movement over much of Europe. The British Isles were not unaffected by these movements of conflict, migration and change, one of the results of which was the emergence of a culture recognizably similar to those of the historical Celts in Central Europe east of the Rhine. The archæological evidence suggests that the immigrations affecting Wessex from *c.* 1000 B.C. onwards (and which we must now consider) had their origin along the Channel coasts westwards of the Seine, and from areas outside the early Celtic world.

Some of our knowledge of these intrusive Deverel-Rimbury people is derived from their burials; these are scattered thickly over Dorset and Hampshire (where they are centred on Christchurch), appearing as multiple cremations in flat cemeteries, in low scraped-up mounds or as secondary burials in older barrows. The cremations were sometimes placed in urns, at other times not, with practically no grave-goods; their numbers in any one cemetery sometimes exceeded a hundred, as in the Rimbury necropolis, an index of settled, peaceful conditions based on an economy no longer wholly dependent on pastoralism or the chase. Three types of urn, when used for the ashes, have been distinguished; the globular, the barrel and the bucket-shaped. Although the details of their derivation are still matters of relative uncertainty and need much more study, the globular urn may well have been derived from the Neolithic and Bronze Age channelled ware of western France. The barrel-shaped urn, often ornamented with straight or horseshoe-shaped, finger-tipped applied bands may owe its origin in part to British Middle Bronze Age styles of pottery. On the other hand, the rough bucket urn is a generalized type of vessel with roots going back to Neolithic and Bronze Age traditions in north-western Europe. Plate 66

The distribution of these urnfields containing ten or more burials thins out considerably northwards as we approach Salisbury, and on Salisbury Plain they are practically non-existent. Here we encounter instead an increasing number of contemporary urns inserted singly as secondary burials in pre-existing barrows, from which it would almost seem as if the inhabitants already in possession of this region had at first raised some sort of barrier against further northward encroachment. Yet this cannot have been entirely the case, since it is on the chalk downlands of Cranborne Chase and of southern and northern Wiltshire that we meet with the other and very much more important manifestation of the Deverel-Rimbury immigrants, their agricultural and stock-breeding activities. But even here it remains a moot point whether this new form of agricultural economy formed part of the originally introduced culture, or whether the ditched and embanked cattle-kraals we have yet to consider were not taken over from the indigenous enclosures of the natives, such as those of the Rams Hill type, and adapted by the immigrants as they slowly penetrated northwards. It is a noteworthy fact, as first pointed out by Mrs. C. M. Piggott, that a marked dichotomy exists when we plot the distribution of major urnfields and of enclosures known to have been constructed and used by these same people. This may, of course, merely mean that we have not as yet discovered traces of such earthworks in the areas of primary settlement. Yet major urnfields are conspicuously absent in the vicinity of many of the enclosures, especially of those on the Marlborough Downs and of those running along the South Downs to Sussex where we first met with the phenomenon, and from which conceivably they could have emanated, to be incorporated later into the Deverel-Rimbury complex.

The enclosures themselves conform to no standard pattern; some are squarish, others have curvilinear sides. They usually range from ¼ to 2 acres in extent and may have single or multiple entrances. Martin Down Camp and South Lodge Camp in Cranborne Chase are the two classic examples; they were excavated by General Pitt-Rivers, who proved them to belong to the Late Bronze Age. A third was identified later on Boscombe Down East closely associated with a complicated system of linear ditches, to be followed by five others on the Marlborough Downs where it was shown that one was earlier and another later than a small squarish field system. The egg-shaped enclosure close to Woodhenge excavated by Mrs. Cunnington probably belongs to the same class.

The area of most intensive Deverel-Rimbury activity so far studied is that of the Bourne Valley running north-eastwards from Salisbury. Both sides of this valley are scored with a complex system of univallate and bivallate V-shaped ditches running at more or less regular intervals down to the river and enclosing large tracts of land which have been interpreted as cattle ranches. These boundary ditches can be seen occasionally to separate areas of pasture; at other times, as on Milston Down, the ditch cuts ruthlessly through a system of fields showing that these must have reverted to pasture at an early date. In some instances it is evident that these ditches were used as cattle-ways separating areas of arable; one runs underneath an Early Iron Age hill-fort on Quarley Hill and so must have preceded it.

Intensification of the field system with attendant ditches in the later Early Iron Age naturally renders dating of certain of the systems hazardous, but there can be no doubt that cultivation by the plough was first introduced by the Deverel-Rimbury people. On Marleycombe Hill, for instance, three Late Bronze Age barrows were found to have been built on top of the edges of fields, whilst at Ebbesbourne Wake a hoard of sixteen contemporary bronze bangles and a bronze torque was discovered buried in a shallow hole in one of a system of small rectangular fields that had early been allowed to revert to grass.

But it was the discovery of the enclosure on Boscombe Down East, actually attached to one of these boundary ditches, that clinched the matter and suggested that these enclosures were kraals for impounding cattle from the ranches. Excavations did not disclose signs of human habitation within, though the encircling ditch yielded much Deverel-Rimbury pottery and bones of horse, dog, pig, sheep and oxen. The appearance of a small breed of horse here and in the Martin Down enclosure shows that this animal was at last taking its place in rural economy.

The subsequent discovery of the remains of an actual farmstead on Thorny Down, some 2½ miles to the south-west of the Boscombe Down enclosure, has added materially to our knowledge of contemporary human settlement. Though situated on uncultivated downland, no surface indications of the remains of dwellings below were visible but for the presence of a few rabbit scrapes containing numerous identifiable potsherds. Almost total excavation of the area produced the outlines of a small compound enclosing discrete groups of post-holes in the chalk and representing some nine small dwellings of a farmer and his family. A number of the holes had been duplicated, suggesting that in process of time replacement of rotted posts had become necessary. The structures seem to have been grouped round a central rectangular-shaped house with porch, Plates 64, 65 and it was noted that the housewife had kept their interiors remarkably clean; most of the objects recovered occurred in the post-holes; probably, during periodical cleaning, rubbish had accumulated in the dark recesses and was subsequently over-looked. Cooking was carried out by roasting in holes with red-hot flints (pot-boilers), and grain, mostly wheat and barley, was ground to flour on saddle-querns. Flint scrapers and knives were still in use as in the Boscombe Down enclosure, the raw material having almost certainly been obtained from the old flint-mines on Easton Down, 2½ miles away, where a contemporary broken pot had been found earlier. Perhaps to bring luck to the community, an old Cornish greenstone axe had been placed in one of the post-holes, whilst a somewhat similar one may have been used for the same purpose in the Boscombe Down kraal.

Spinning and weaving of wool occupied part of the attention of the women of the house, who must have possessed an upright loom, as cylindrical clay loom weights were found in the principal house, similar to those found with spindle whorls in comparable sites in Sussex and in a strange pit at Swanwick in Hampshire which may have been a pitfall trap with a pointed stake at its base. The nearest source of water (apart from rain-water) was the river Bourne 2 miles away.

This picture of relatively primitive life must not, however, blind us to the fact that more developed and costly articles were now becoming available to the farmer and his wife. In this case, by some mishap the farmer's wife had broken her bronze ribbed bracelet in her inner room and left the pieces on the floor, whilst her husband had carelessly mislaid his double-looped bronze spearhead behind the house. He may even have been thoughtless enough to have laid aside and lost his valuable leaf-shaped bronze sword, for one such was subsequently found, two thousand years later, on the site of Figsbury Rings less than a mile away.

Bronze smiths and tinkers were now actively plying their wares and skill, and without doubt their visits were eagerly anticipated at these isolated farmsteads. Nevertheless, their trade seems to have been a somewhat hazardous one, otherwise we should not so frequently find their hoards buried to await their return from some extended journey. Actually few founder's hoards have been recovered from the heart of Wessex; the few that have been found are confined mostly to areas of known Deverel-Rimbury occupation. Thus, one of nine socketed axes comes from Manton Down near Marlborough, and another containing six of Breton type from Nether Wallop in Hampshire. At the headwaters of the River Ebble, apparently on a trade route to Somerset and the West, three hoards of interest have been found relatively close together. One large one at Donhead St. Mary contained eight winged axes of West Alpine type, three socketed axes and a bronze mould, a socketed hammer and gouge drill, a large bronze ring and bundles of wire. A small one at Ansty Hollow near Alvediston produced a socketed axe and some broken scraps, whilst the hoard of sixteen bronze bangles and a torque or neck ornament of northern European derivation, which we have already noted, was found along the same ancient trackway at Ebbesbourne Wake. Another hoard of a torque and bracelets was found at Lake in Wiltshire. Plate 67

Two similar cast bronze twisted torques and a bronze looped pin found with a clay loom-weight and fragments of a globular urn from another Deverel-Rimbury settlement at Plaitford, Hampshire, have raised points of interest. It is now accepted that the production of such torques, pins and ribbed bracelets of the Thorny Down type, once they had been introduced into Britain, became a speciality of a Late Bronze Age industry centred in Somerset, where they are well known in such remarkable hoards as those from Edington Burtle, Monkswood near Bath, and West Buckland amongst others. From this centre they were peddled to Dorset, Wiltshire, Hampshire and even to Sussex. Long looped pins imply adoption of the Continental method of fastening clothing; no longer were V-perforated buttons considered *de rigueur:* the 'waistcoat age', as it has been jocularly called, had ended.

The monopoly, too, of these skilled workers in bronze was now in sight, and much of their livelihood was very shortly to be snatched from them by the blacksmith. The outstanding properties of iron as a material for weapons and edge-tools, and its ready availability, had already effected a profound change in the economic life of the Continent; by 500 B.C. a slow trickle of iron objects from across the Channel presaged momentous events that were again to transform the face of Wessex and the southern counties. Technological progress had at last mastered this new and indispensable metal; the blacksmith entered the field, leaving the bronze worker's output restricted to objects other than edge-tools.

Far away in the Mediterranean, the Greeks of the Periclean Age concerned themselves with their own affairs, too remote, materially and intellectually, to cast an eye on barbarian Britain; Rome was engaged in dispute with the Sabines. Yet both these powers were, in the immediate sequel, to produce indirectly very marked changes in the economic and artistic life of Wessex, and to demonstrate once again the dependence of the north on the civilizing influences of the south. To their influence on Britain is to be added that of a third and more barbarous people, The Celts. With their arrival, at the beginning of what is archæologically the Early Iron Age, Wessex and the rest of the British Isles move into a new phase. But to round off the story of pre-Celtic Wessex, we must, in an epilogue, consider the outlines of this Celtic episode before the Roman Conquest.

CHAPTER XII

Epilogue: Celtic Wessex

ALTHOUGH SPORADIC MIGRATION to our eastern and southern shores continued throughout the Late Bronze Age, the first clear-cut evidence of intensification of folk-movements into Wessex does not become apparent until the fourth century B.C. when, perhaps as a result of population pressure and land hunger, groups of Celtic-speaking and farming communities from north-western France, their material culture a version of the Hallstatt Cultures of the Continent, settled on our coasts at such sites as Hengistbury Head at the mouth of the Hampshire Avon, and farther inland on the chalk downs. A climatic change (from the relatively dry Sub-Boreal, to the wetter Sub-Atlantic period) may have been broadly contemporary with such migration and may indeed have been a partial cause, as the chalk uplands might be regarded as now fit for more intense and concentrated tillage. In any event, we find from now onwards and until the Roman Conquest, rapid and widespread expansion of downland settlement to the point of almost complete saturation. The settlers themselves seem to have met with no obvious resistance from their Late Bronze Age relatives already in occupation and, at first, ample room must have been available for all to co-exist peacefully. No sites have yet been recognized on which continuity of occupation can be claimed, though it may be suspected in certain instances.

It would be wrong to minimize the complexity of the movements and interactions of the various groups of Early Iron Age peoples and their manifestations in the south of Britain; a whole book could well be devoted to this most fascinating and formative period of prehistory when, in the sequel, we shall meet for the first time with peoples and places whose names have actually survived historical record. No longer shall we have to rely wholly on cultural debris discarded by illiterate communities. But at first we have to depend solely on archæological evidence and to that we must revert, though only a very brief sketch can here be attempted, as epilogue to our main story.

The farmsteads of the earliest settlers have certain features in common that distinguish them sharply from those of the preceding Late Bronze Age; they are clearly dependent on radically new and more advanced forms of agricultural economy. Whilst stock-breeding and occasional hunting supplemented the fare, cereals grown on a new scale unquestionably formed the bulk of their produce. Stable conditions appear soon to have been established and, with capital invested wholly in land, much of the downland landscape must eventually have assumed the form of a patchwork of small squarish fields cultivated by the two-ox plough, now mostly obliterated by later cultivation but still largely visible and traceable on aerial photographs.

The cereals grown included Emmer wheat, hulled barley, various forms of oats and chess and, amongst innovations, rye and a completely new form of wheat known as Spelt *(Triticum spelta)*. The introduction of this new cereal is of considerable importance, as it goes far to explain hitherto puzzling features found in these farmsteads such as the not infrequent finds of carbonized grain associated with the remains of baking ovens and great heaps of ashes and burnt flints. Now, these deposits indicate some essential agricultural process which H. Helbaek has convincingly shown to have been connected with the threshing of Spelt. Grains of Spelt are clamped so tightly in their husks as to be impossible to thresh unless the spikelets have been first rendered fragile by baking. Occasional accidents would have caused some of the grain to become overheated and burnt.

The harvested grain had now to be stored. A selected portion for the coming year's seed was placed in reserve in rat-proof granaries built on platforms held on four posts above ground, whilst the bulk for use was buried in containers below ground in deep, carefully dug storage-pits covered by some sort of lid. These storage-pits are very numerous on all farmsteads so far examined, though their contents and state of preservation do not suggest that many were in use at any one time. Not only did they attract vermin, but the damp climate and moist chalk walls favoured the growth of moulds and bacteria which soon caused them to become fouled. When this happened, clean fresh pits were immediately dug, and the old ones filled in with the freshly excavated chalk and any other domestic refuse found lying about on the farm. They were not, as was previously supposed, human dwelling-pits.

Life in these farms must have been active at all seasons of the year. The grain was ground on saddle-querns and the flour used for baking cakes and buns. Spindle-whorls, decorated bone combs and loom-weights prove that weaving of cloth had now become an essential occupation, though we know nothing of probable dyeing processes to render clothing more attractive. Besides the use of iron tools and implements, the farmer and his wife were now able to deck themselves with bronze brooches and bracelets, glass beads, and decorated armlets hand-cut from Kimmeridge shale. In the evenings they were able to amuse themselves with games employing decorated bone counters. Their furniture has not survived; but there is no reason to deny them stools, cupboards and tables, and basketry almost certainly entered into their home industries.

As at all times and in all places, pottery looms large as an index of changing peoples and traditions. And so it is that in these early farmsteads we find new wares: some of the coarser varieties have features based on Late Bronze Age traditions but include new shouldered forms derived from the Hallstatt bronze situla; others are of a very much finer kind, bowl-shaped, furrowed initially but in the later phases incised after firing, and covered with a bright red burnished hæmatite slip to imitate the colour of bronze. The inclusion of this attractive hæmatite ware, concentrated largely in Wessex northwards from the harbours of the Hampshire and Dorset coasts, must have glowed alluringly in the evening fire-light and added appreciably to the farm-wife's delight. Their uniformity of style and shape strongly suggests that many were made at one place and marketed over a wide area.

Our knowledge of the farm buildings in Wessex is confined to one almost completely excavated example, that of Little Woodbury about 1½ miles south of Salisbury. This farmstead with its associated storage-pits and other features was partly examined and most exhaustively interpreted by G. Bersu for the Prehistoric Society in 1938-39. Here the post-holes of a large circular wooden house, about 45 feet in diameter with entrance porch, were found towards the centre of a palisaded enclosure; but whether this was typical of contemporary buildings must for the present remain an open question. Little can be said of any form of internal partitioning; but the roof of the farmhouse was probably thatched.

Plate 68

Clusters of storage-pits suggestive of similar isolated farmsteads occur in great numbers especially in southern Wiltshire and over the border in Hampshire, but none has been so carefully explored as that of Little Woodbury. All Cannings Cross near Devizes, the type-site of the culture, was the first to be recognized, and its large extent suggested the makings of a village rather than that of a single farm. The existence of larger agricultural units thus implied was confirmed in 1948-49 during levelling operations on Boscombe Down aerodrome when closely spaced pits, ditches and working hollows were found to cover an area of some 76 acres. Continuity of settlement was here remarkable in that it was proved to have covered some 800 years from the very beginning of the Early Iron Age right through to the end of the Romano-British period. A conservative rural economy and an apparent freedom from political upheavals for the majority were here strikingly evident and indicate the underlying strength and tenacity of settlement in Wessex at the time, though no doubt inter-tribal skirmishes and cattle-raiding relieved monotony.

The conservatism of the peasants and their stubborn provincialism, with so much capital sunk in land, was in fact the keynote and strength of the Wessex Early Iron Age throughout the greater part of its history; it was almost certainly the direct cause of the diversion of aggressive raiders to other parts of Britain about 250 B.C. A war-scare from across the Channel suddenly threatened our southern coasts and, no doubt with a frenzy that all can understand, the farmsteads were strengthened by digging deep defensive ditches around them, as at Little Woodbury, whilst, by concerted action, massive earthen hill-forts were constructed on numerous commanding hill-tops. The great contour hill-forts of Wessex are indeed one of its grandest and most impressive features, and it is now generally agreed that the majority of the simpler univallate type, such as those of Quarley Hill, Figsbury Rings and the earlier phases of Maiden Castle and Yarnbury Castle, were built at this time as temporary camps of refuge rather than as permanent living quarters, though occupation has been attested in some. Resistance on such a scale proved effective and the scare seems to have rapidly subsided, as some of the forts were left unfinished as that on Ladle Hill in Hampshire; so was the defensive ditch surrounding Little Woodbury.

Plates 69, 70

This attempted invasion of our southern coasts is likely to have been caused by an eruption of bands of warlike Celtic chieftains living in the Marne region. Their panoply of war, including war chariots, was now more elaborate and we know that they were also active patrons of new forms of Celtic art. The old Hallstatt Culture had gradually given place to that of La Tène, a brilliant Celtic culture that had arisen north of the Alps as a direct result of barbarian commercial contacts down the Rhône with the prosperous and well-established Greek colony at Massilia (Marseilles) and with the Etruscans of Italy, tempered perhaps with other contributions from such sources as the Scythians of eastern Europe. In return for numerous products from the North, including tin and slaves, these civilized Mediterranean centres were now flooding Gaul with a host of new articles; jars of wine, metal table services and other desirable objects appealing to barbarian fancy. And many of these were highly decorated in conventionalized classical style. Celtic artist-craftsmen, quick to appreciate the potentialities of new designs and styles, were not content to copy them slavishly. Their genius lay in other directions; artistry in their hands, especially in metal-work, became transformed and transmuted to heights that have rarely if ever been equalled and which was later to flower so conspicuously in other parts of the British Isles.

Thus well equipped and ripe for trouble, these chieftains from the Marne sought adventure across the Channel. Temporary lodgment was apparently effected on Hengistbury Head, but the main weight of invasion was concentrated in Sussex and in east Yorkshire. In the latter region the tribal name of the Parisi betokens their place of origin, and there they implanted the first seeds of Celtic art which inspired the exquisite metal-work with its abstract motifs that was to have so far-reaching an effect in these islands in subsequent years.

The Wessex peasantry for their part appear to have settled down to two further centuries of relative and uninspired peace, content to continue their humdrum farming activities and to absorb by slow infiltration minor cultural traits, mainly ceramic, from the surrounding districts but not, as pointed out by Sir Mortimer Wheeler, embracing tangible exports or imports. One might say that these dull, unenterprising peasant communities, in seeking security, and with a misplaced conception of freedom, unconsciously diverted the seeds of a higher culture from their doors: they made Wessex, however, the granary of Iron Age Britain and by so doing enabled the Roman Province to establish its civil settlement on a firm agricultural basis.

For, on both the western and eastern boundaries of Wessex, events were shaping that foreshadowed foreign domination. Certainly from the beginning of the second century B.C. and probably earlier, the tin trade between Cornwall and Brittany, for ultimate passage down the Loire or Garonne to the Massiliot Greek merchants, was passing through the hands of the Veneti, a powerful seafaring Gaulish tribe occupying north-western France. The close relations thereby established, not unmixed with tribal skirmishes and successful endeavours on the part of the Veneti to gain a firmer foothold in Cornwall, inevitably resulted in cultural interchange. New methods of defence invariably accompany new weapons of offence, and the Veneti were noted and skilled users of the sling, a more deadly long-range weapon than the spear. Safety from its penetrating power could be obtained only by increasing the distance between combatants, and this was accomplished by the development in Brittany of new forms of fortification distinguished by the possession of multiple ramparts. Complex forts and cliff-castles based on these prototypes now appear in Cornwall and gradually spread, with probable Venetic settlement, inland and up the coasts of the Severn where we find great stone-girt multivallate forts such as those of Worlebury above Weston-super-Mare enclosing 10½ acres, and Dolebury on the Mendips (22½ acres).

It is now generally agreed that the year 56 B.C. marks an important turning-point in the fortunes of Wessex. History records that it was during this year that Julius Cæsar inflicted his resounding defeat of the Veneti of Brittany both on sea and land and that, to teach the Gauls a lesson, all who had not perished were sold into slavery. Now this event has been very plausibly equated by Wheeler with the sudden appearance on our Dorset and Hampshire coasts of refugees and fugitive chieftains who had survived the disaster and who had, in their hour of need, appealed to their relatives in Britain for help. On Hengistbury Head we find the remains of their domestic ware; an iron anchor and chain probably of similar origin was found in Bulbury Camp near Poole Harbour. But these immigrants are best represented at Maiden Castle in Dorset, already inhabited by Wessex peasantry within a small univallate fortress, there to make it their tribal home and headquarters. Wheeler's extensive and illuminating excavations have shown that it was very probably at this time that the fortress assumed its present revolutionary shape in the hands of a master-mind, necessitating total remodelling on a colossal scale and embodying stupendous multiple ramparts and outworks designed to keep the defenders out of effective sling-range. Large hoards of up to 22,260 sling-stones were in fact found during excavations at strategic points within the defences.

The sudden introduction into Wessex of this new form of defensive military architecture, closely linked with the appearance of bead-rim pots, simulating metal prototypes, countersunk handles and rotary querns, may be taken to imply the intrusion of a military minority of Breton origin sufficiently strong to achieve effective political domination and to secure a major labour force for the construction of defensive works. Their dominion or overlordship seems finally to have embraced a very large part of Wessex, by which time the tribe had become known as the Durotriges; it had considerable political control and its own coinage based on that of Gaul.

Plate 71

We now find old forts being reconstructed and new ones being built on the multivallate principle. We have only to recall such well-known forts as those of Badbury Rings, Hod Hill, Hambledon Hill, Yarnbury Castle, Battlesbury Camp,

Danebury and Sidbury Hill amongst others, to appreciate the insecurity and tenseness of these troublous times. Though few have been excavated, we may nevertheless be justified in ascribing all to this late period. Hambledon Hill is of special interest, as it is still possible to see the remains of house-platforms within its inner ramparts. Plate 70

The necessity for building so many forts on such a scale is now considered to have been connected with new dangers that threatened the eastern boundaries of Wessex. By 50 B.C. much more formidable invaders, the Belgæ, from northern Gaul, had conquered south-eastern Britain and their sway extended westwards through Hampshire practically to the River Test. The line of multivallate defence works, including Danebury and Bury Hill, up this valley and northwards, has been interpreted by Professor Hawkes as a barrier of frontier forts built by Wessex sub-tribes to keep at bay these invaders under Commius, a prince of the Atrebates. For a time they proved availing, but slowly the advance westwards continued until, by about A.D. 10-25, the greater part of Wiltshire, Hampshire and possibly parts of Dorset had been occupied by these new masters. Belgic wheel-turned pottery and imported Gallo-Belgic wares now become superimposed on the cruder wares of the natives who, at Boscombe Down, Rotherley and Woodcuts, amongst other places, continued to pursue their old rural occupations and seem to have accepted the position in preference to eviction. But other farmsteads, as that of Little Woodbury, had already been abandoned.

We must not forget to notice, however, one small enclave of people of outstanding interest who had by 50 B.C. or a little earlier settled amongst the inhospitable marshes and lakes of Somerset on artificially made islands or crannogs, no doubt for security. The lake-dwellings at Glastonbury and Meare have been for more than 50 years systematically examined by A. Bulleid and H. St. G. Gray and have thereby become famous for the very complete picture of contemporary life thus obtained and so fortunately preserved in wet, peaty soil. That at Glastonbury is the more complete. Within a palisaded enclosure of just over 2 acres the whole surface of the peat had been covered by a platform of logs and brushwood on which were built some eighty-nine circular buildings with artificially laid clay floors. As these floors sank, new layers of clay were added; in one dwelling ten superimposed floors with baked clay hearths were encountered. A specially made causeway led from the village to drier ground for wheeled traffic, while dug-out canoes were available for water transport and fowling. The finds in so favourable a situation were exceptionally rich and included numerous skilfully made and decorated tools, weapons, receptacles and ornaments of bronze, tin, lead, iron, wood, bone, glass, jet and Kimmeridge shale. Industries included weaving, *Fig. 22* potting and metal-working, and gambling with dice appears to have been a favourite pastime. Milling was carried out with rotary querns. The whole culture in fact represents a society of artist-craftsmen engaged in trade, including the use of Dobunnic iron currency-bars, and living a very much more elevated and richer life than that of the downland farmers with whom there seems to have been little or no contact except possibly southwards to Dorset and Maiden Castle.

The clue to the origin of this small group of people, who also at times inhabited the Mendip caves and the hill-fort of Worlebury, almost certainly lies in the great quantities of sling-stones at their disposal and their highly ornamented, attractively incised La Tène pottery which is paralleled in Brittany. It is reasonable to assume that we have here a small group of settlers founded on the old Cornish-Breton tin trade—possibly Strabo's Venetic emporium—and later augmented considerably by Venetic refugee families who had managed to escape the wrath of Cæsar. But their escape was short-lived. Being less acquiescent towards new masters, their end came in massacre, as at

Worlebury, and this is more likely to have been due to conflict with the Belgæ than with the Roman legionaries.

The Belgic state and its sphere of influence had long been a thorn in the flesh of the Romans and so, with the death of King Cunobelin, the chance was seized by the Emperor Claudius in A.D. 43 to subdue for ever these unruly barbarians. Having conquered and consolidated their position in the south-east, the Second Augustan Legion under the future Emperor Vespasian struck west demolishing in their advance, amongst other pockets of resistance, the singly ditched Belgic enclosure at Bury Hill and the doubly entrenched plateau-fort on Boscombe Down West. The final active defence of the Durotrigian capital and stronghold at Maiden Castle, with its hurriedly but carefully dug war cemetery at its gates, has been graphically described by Wheeler. This is no place to discuss subsequent

Fig. 22 Decorated pots from Glastonbury, Somerset. Height of smaller pot 4½ in., larger pot 8¼ in.

events, except to recall that the Romanization of the downland farmsteads and villages must have followed rapidly. Their gleaming fields of corn must soon have attracted the attention of the Roman invaders. As far as we can judge at present, Salisbury Plain and Cranborne Chase were turned, without interruption, into Imperial Estates with administrative head-quarters possibly at Sorviodunum (Old Sarum) and Badbury Rings for the main purpose of feeding the army of occupation.

Native deities would have continued to be worshipped, even if assimilated to Roman types, and on the hill-side at Cerne Abbas in Dorset there still survives one of the most remarkable representations of a pagan god north of the Alps—a huge figure of a phallic, club-bearing giant, over 200 feet high and cut into the turf-covered chalk of the steeply-sloping hill. While the conventions of the figure suggest Roman provincial art, and an assimilation to the Hercules type, it must nevertheless represent a local cult-centre of native origin.

Plate 72

Here we must leave Wessex, brooding on its apparent mis-fortunes and stubbornly conserving its strength—a Wessex still unsuspecting a later act of Imperial administration that was to turn its rich farmlands into sheep-walks, unaware of the disastrous Saxon invasions in store, and of its final and glorious rebirth under Alfred the Great which was destined to turn Wessex pre-history into English history.

Bibliography

GENERAL WORKS

DOBSON, D. P. *The Archaeology of Somerset* (1931).

HELBAEK, H. Early Crops in Southern England. *Proc. Prehist. Soc.*, XVIII (1952), 194.

PEAKE, H. J. E. *The Archaeology of Berkshire* (1931).

PIGGOTT, S. Archaeology in Wessex, I–III. *Arch. News Letter*, IV (1951–2), 33, 65, 113.

PIGGOTT, S. AND HAWKES, C. F. C. *Victoria County History of Wiltshire*, Vol. I, Part I (forthcoming).

TRATMAN, E. K. The Prehistoric Archaeology of the Bristol Region. Chap. IX of *Bristol and its Adjoining Counties* (1955).

CHAPTER I

RANKINE, W. F. Stone 'Maceheads' with Mesolithic associations in S.E. England. *Proc. Prehist. Soc.*, XV (1949), 70.

RANKINE, W. F. Mesolithic Research in Southern England. *Arch. News Letter*, V (1954), 37.

RANKINE, W. F. Mesolithic Finds in Wiltshire. *Wilts. Arch. Mag.*, LVI (1955), 149.

SUMMERS, P. G. A Mesolithic Site near Iwerne Minster, Dorset. *Proc. Prehist. Soc.*, VII (1941), 145.

CHAPTERS II–V

PIGGOTT, S. *The Neolithic Cultures of the British Isles* (1954), with full bibliography.

PIGGOTT, S. Windmill Hill—East or West? *Proc. Prehist. Soc.*, XXI (1955), 96.

STONE, J. F. S. AND WALLIS, F. S. Third Report of the Sub-Committee . . . on the Petrological Examination of Stone Axes. *Proc. Prehist. Soc.*, XVII (1951), 99.

CHAPTER VI

CALKIN, J. B. The Bournemouth Area in Neolithic and Early Bronze Age Times. *Proc. Dorset N.H. and Arch. Soc.,* LXXIII (1951), 32.

PIGGOTT, S. AND C. M. Excavation of Barrows on Crichel and Launceston Downs, Dorset. *Arch.*, XC (1944), 47.

PIGGOTT, S. A Trepanned Skull of the Beaker Period from Dorset . . . *Proc. Prehist Soc.,* VI (1940), 112.

PIGGOTT, S. AND C. M. The Excavation of a Barrow on Rockbourne Down, Hants. *Proc. Hants F.C. and Arch. Soc.,* XVI (1946), 156.

PIGGOTT, C. M. Excavation of Fifteen Barrows in the New Forest . . . *Proc. Prehist. Soc.,* IX (1943), 1.

STEVENS, F. AND STONE, J. F. S. The Barrows of Winterslow. *Wilts. Arch. Mag.,* XLVIII (1938), 174.

STONE, J. F. S. A Settlement Site of the Beaker Period on Easton Down . . . *Wilts. Arch. Mag.,* XLV (1931), 366.

STONE, J. F. S. A Case of Bronze Age Cephalotaphy on Easton Down. *Man,* 1934, No. 51.

STONE, J. F. S. An Early Bronze Age Grave in Fargo Plantation . . . *Wilts. Arch. Mag.,* XLVIII (1938), 357.

STONE, J. F. S., AND HILL, N. G. A Round Barrow on Stockbridge Down, Hampshire. *Ant. Journ.,* XX (1940), 39.

WILLIAMS, A. Bronze Age Barrows on Charmy Down and Lansdown. Somerset. *Ant. Journ.,* XXX (1950), 34.

CHAPTERS VII AND VIII

ATKINSON, R. J. C. *et al. Excavations at Dorchester, Oxon: First Report* (1951), Chap. VIII, with full bibliography.

ATKINSON, R. J. C. *Stonehenge* (1956).

CUNNINGTON, M. E. The 'Sanctuary' on Overton Hill, near Avebury. *Wilts. Arch. Mag.,* XLV (1931), 300.

CUNNINGTON, M. E. *Woodhenge* (1929).

STONE, J. F. S., PIGGOTT, S. AND BOOTH, A. ST. J. Durrington Walls, Wiltshire . . . *Ant. Journ.,* XXXIV (1954), 155.

TAYLOR, C., AND TRATMAN, E. K. The Priddy Circles. *Proc. Univ. Bristol Speaeo Soc.,* VII (1957), 7.

CHAPTERS IX AND X

APSIMON, A. M. Dagger Graves of the 'Wessex' Early Bronze Age. *Univ. Lond. Inst. Arch. Ann. Report*, X (1954), 37.

ATKINSON, R. J. C. *et al.* A Pond Barrow at Winterbourne Steepleton, Dorset. *Arch. Journ.*, XVIII (1952), 1.

DE NAVARRO, J. M. The British Isles and the Beginning of the Northern Bronze Age. *Early Cultures of N.W. Europe* (1950), Chap. V.

PIGGOTT, S. The Early Bronze Age in Wessex. *Proc. Prehist. Soc.*, IV (1938), 52.

PIGGOTT, S. AND C. M. Excavations on Ram's Hill, Berks. *Ant. Journ.*, XX (1940), 467.

STONE, J. F. S. AND THOMAS, L. C. The Use and Distribution of Faience in the Ancient East and Prehistoric Europe. *Proc. Prehist. Soc.*, XXII (1956), 37.

STONE, J. F. S. A Middle Bronze Age Urnfield on Easton Down, Winterslow. *Wilts. Arch. Mag.*, XLVI (1933), 218.

CHAPTER XI

HAWKES, C. F. C., AND PRESTON, J. P. Three Bronze Age Barrows on the Cloven Way. *Ant. Journ.*, XII (1933), 414.

HAWKES, C. F. C. The Deverel Urn and the Picardy Pin. *Proc. Prehist. Soc.*, VIII (1942), 26.

HAWKES, C. F. C. Excavations at Quarley Hill, 1938. *Proc. Hants F.C. and Arch. Soc.*, XIV (1939), 136.

PIGGOTT, C. M. A Middle Bronze Age Barrow and Deverel-Rimbury Urnfield at Latch Farm . . . *Proc. Prehist. Soc.*, IV (1938), 169.

PIGGOTT, C. M. Five Late Bronze Age Enclosures in North Wiltshire. *Proc. Prehist. Soc.*, VIII (1942), 48.

SHORTT, H. DE S. A Hoard of Bangles from Ebbesbourne Wake . . . *Wilts. Arch. Mag.*, LIII (1949), 104.

CHAPTER XII

BERSU, G. Excavations at Little Woodbury, Wiltshire (Part I). *Proc. Prehist. Soc.*, VI (1940), 30.

BRAILSFORD, J., Excavations at Little Woodbury, Wiltshire (Parts II–V). *Proc. Prehist. Soc.*, XIV (1948); *ibid* XV (1949), 156.

CHAPTER XII—*continued*

CUNNINGTON, M. E. *All Cannings Cross* (1923).
HAWKES, C. F. C. Hill-Forts. *Ant.*, V (1931), 60.
HAWKES, C. F. C. Britons, Romans and Saxons round Salisbury and in Cranborne Chase. *Arch. Journ.*, CIV (1947), 27.
WHEELER, R. E. M. *Maiden Castle, Dorset*, 1943.

SOURCES OF ILLUSTRATIONS

The line illustrations and maps are either original drawings, or re-drawn from published illustrations by the author, except for Figs. 10, 11, 12, 17, which are the work of Mrs. C. D. Fergusson of the School of Scottish Studies, University of Edinburgh.

The photographs for the plates are by Malcolm Murray, Department of Prehistoric Archæology, University of Edinburgh, except for the following: Aerofilms, Plate 32; British Museum, Plates 34, 52, 55, 56; Crown Copyright, Plates 26, 37, 69, 70, 72; E. Cecil Curwen, Plate 51; Dorchester Museum, Plates 43, 44, 45, 46; Alexander Keiller, Plates 1, 2, 3, 4; Newbury Museum, Plates 21, 22; Salisbury Museum, Plate 71; Edwin Smith, Plate 29; *Southern Journal*, Plate 30; J. F. S. Stone, Plates 5, 9, 12, 20, 23, 27, 28, 31, 33, 35, 36, 58, 59.

1

2

3

4

5

6

9

10

1

2

13

4

15

16

17

18

19

20

21

22

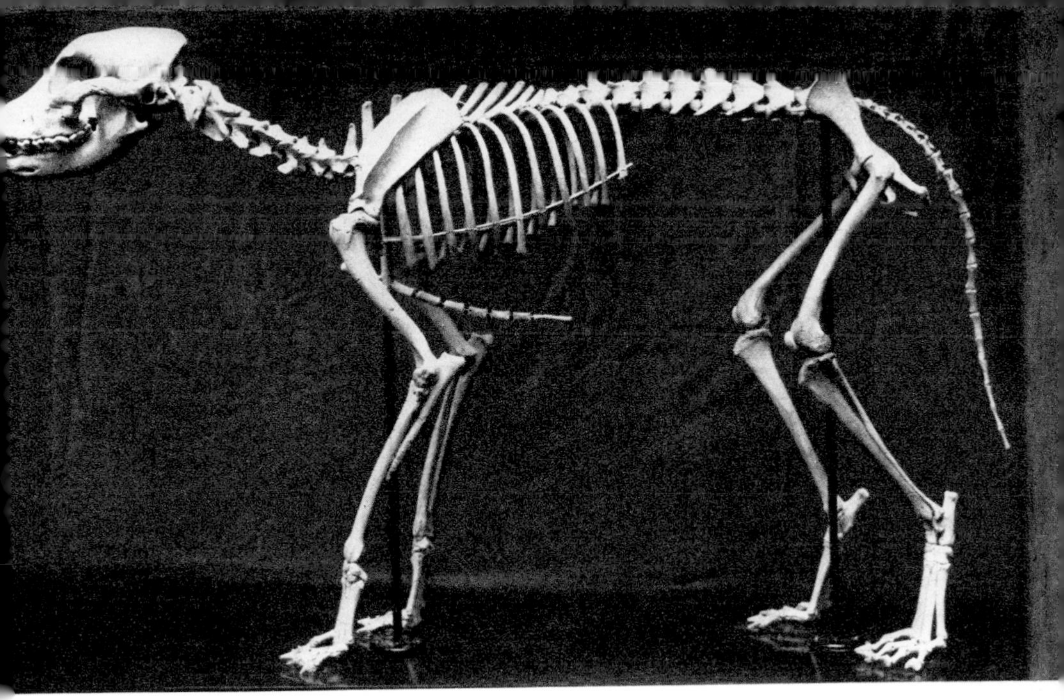

3

25

26

27

28

9

30

31

33

34

35

36

38

39

40

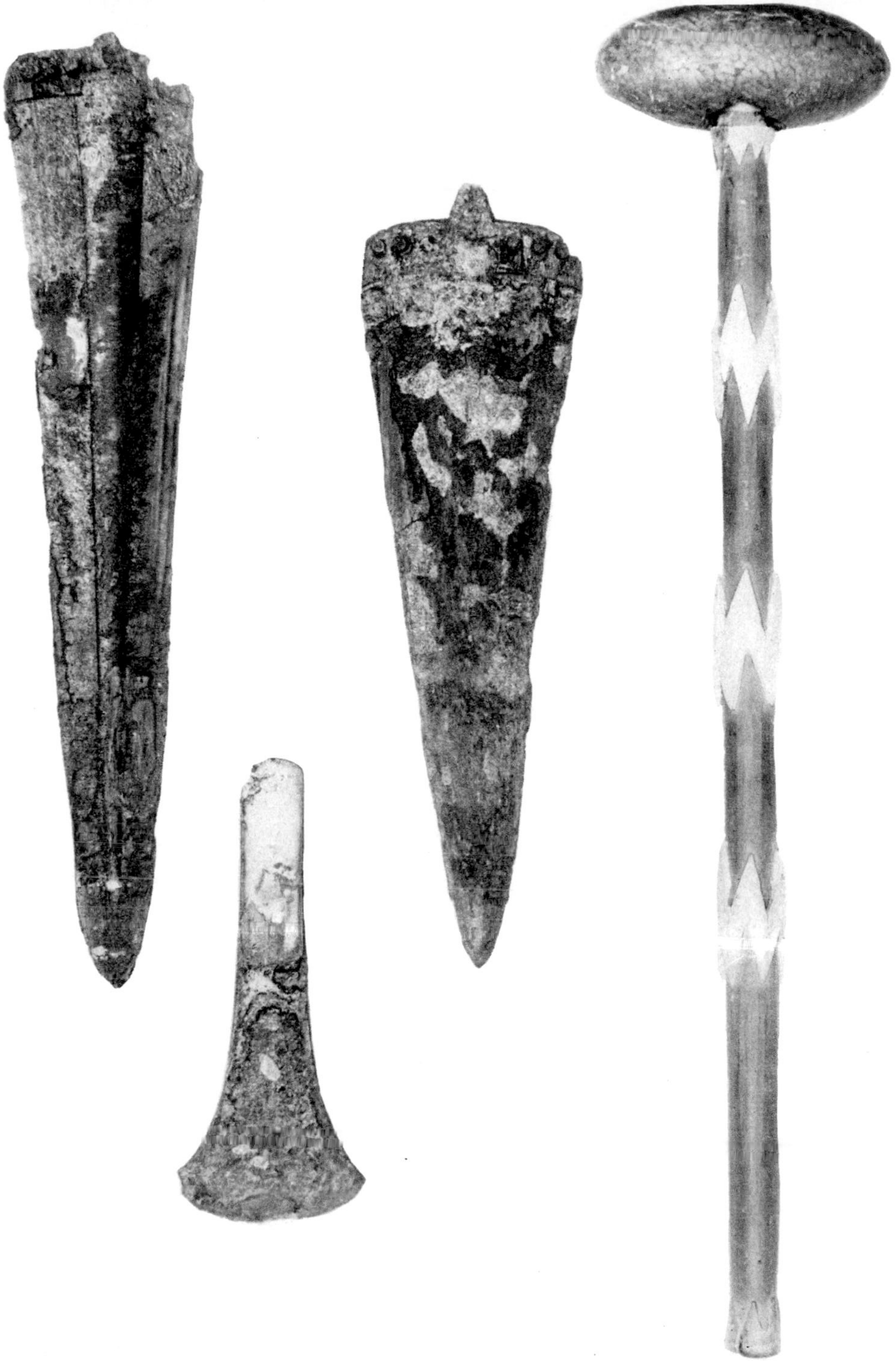

42

45

46

47

48

49

50

51

52

53

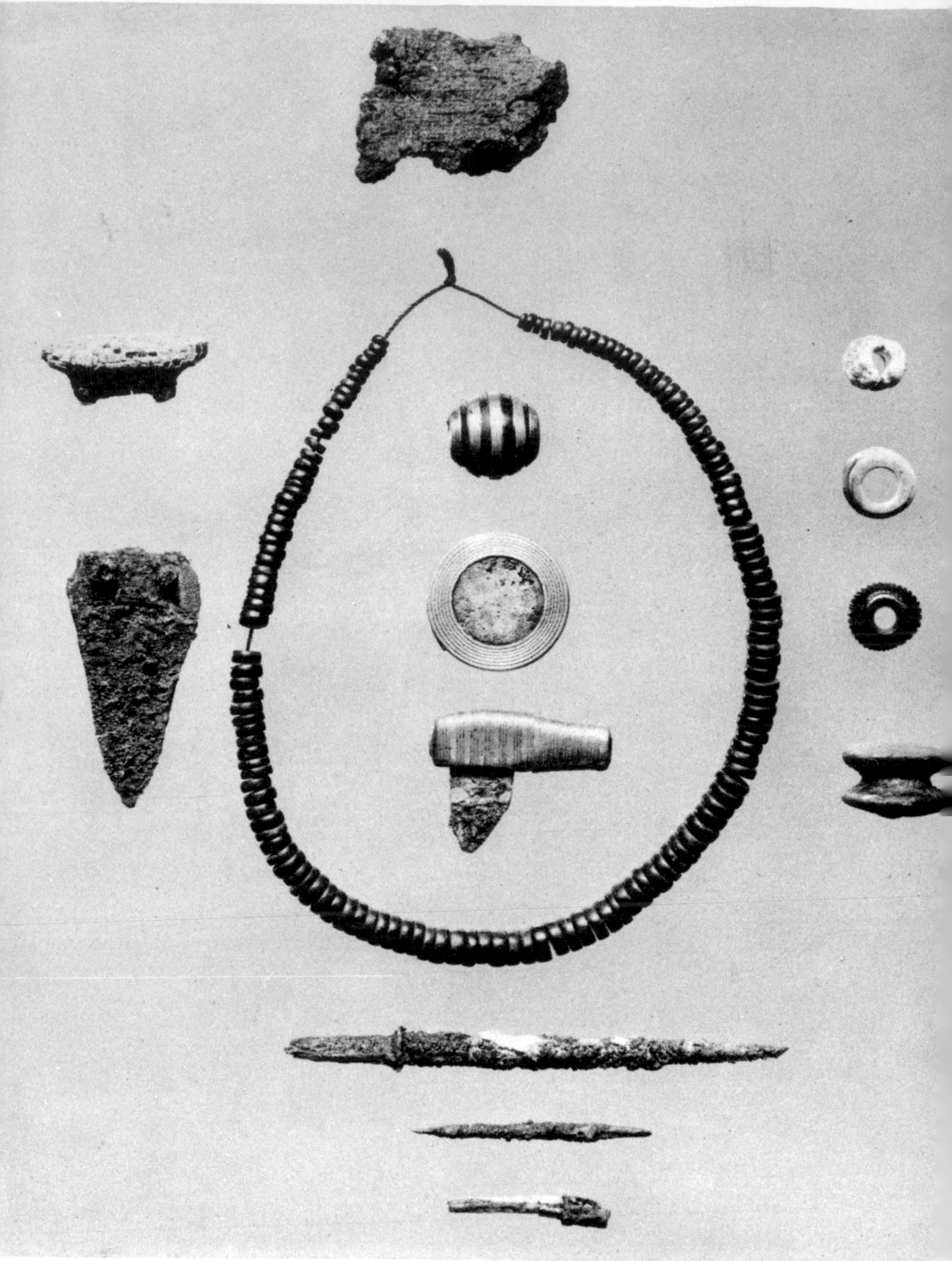

55

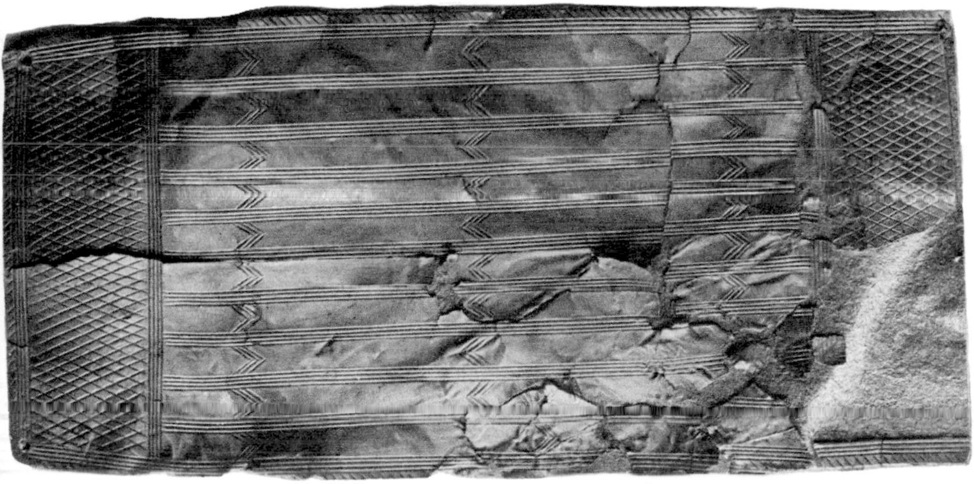
56

57

58

59

60

61

62

63

64

65

66

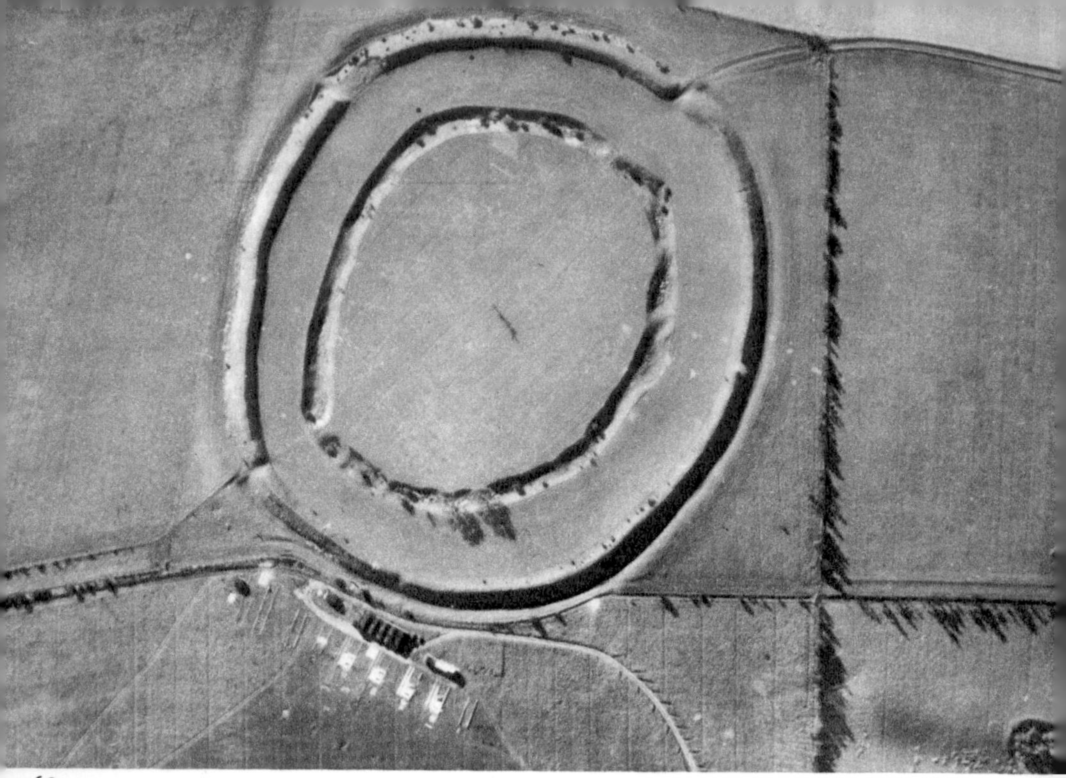

69

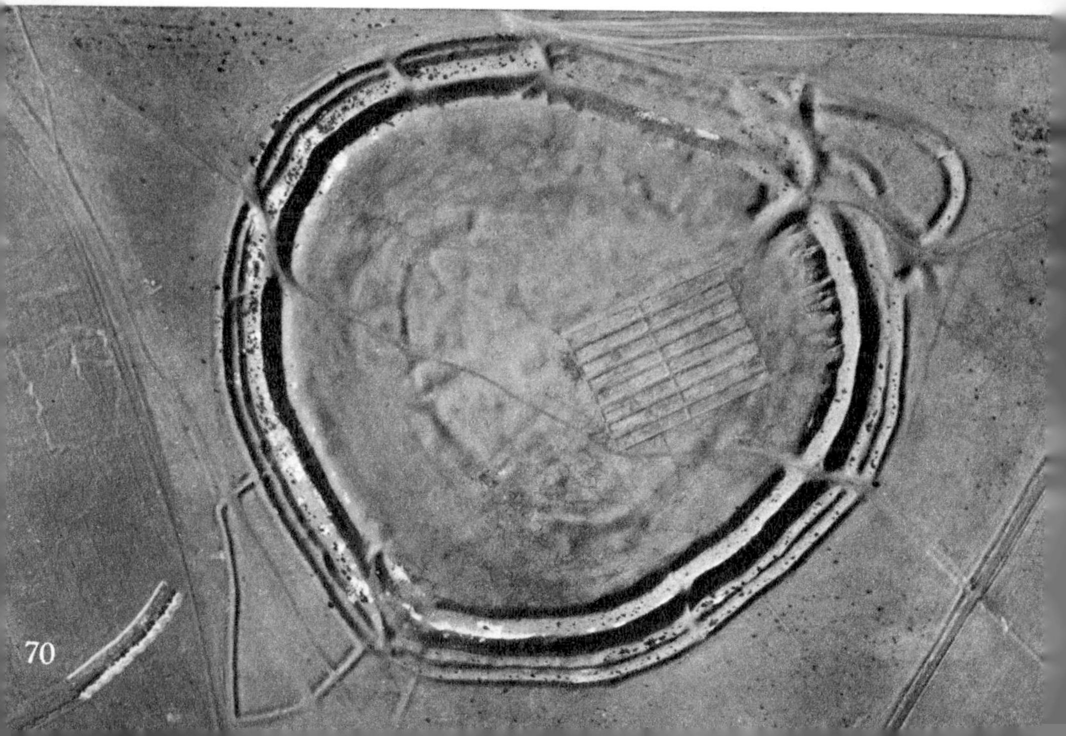

70

71

Notes on the Plates

1–4 Four bowls of Neolithic pottery from the lower levels of the ditches at Windmill Hill. No. 1 is 6 in. diameter at the mouth. Avebury Museum.

5 View of the East Kennet Long Barrow, from the north.

6 View of the frontal façade of the West Kennet Long Barrow after excavation and reconstruction, 1956, looking north towards Silbury Hill in the background.

7 View inside the passage of the West Kennet Long Barrow, after excavation, 1956, looking west into the terminal burial chamber.

8 Primary burials in the south-west chamber ot the West Kennet Long Barrow, 1955.

9 View of the flint-mine shaft on Easton Down during excavation, 1930.

10 Axe-blade of polished jadeite from Breamore, Hants. 8 in. long. Devizes Museum.

11 Vessel of Rinyo-Clacton ware, from the settlement site adjacent to Durrington Walls, Wilts. Height 5½ in. Salisbury Museum.

12 Axe-hammer or battle-axe with shaft-hole, made of stone from the Prescelly Mountains, Pembrokeshire, found at Fifield Bavant, Wilts. Length 9 in. Private collection (cast in Salisbury Museum).

13 Objects with burials under a round barrow at Upton Lovel, Wilts. Above are bone points and a graduated series of bone objects probably serving as a collar or fringe to a garment; below are stone objects including (centre) a grooved shaft-smoother and (right) a stone battle-axe. The largest bone object in the collar is 7½ in. long. Devizes Museum.

14 Bell-beaker found inverted and almost intact in the uppermost layers of the filling of the north-west chamber in the West Kennet Long Barrow. Height 7½ in. Devizes Museum.

15 Bell-beaker from an inhumation grave at Normanton, Wilts. Height 7¼ in. Devizes Museum.

16 Necked Beaker from grave at Durrington, Wilts. Height 7½ in. Devizes Museum.

17 Gold disc from Early Bronze Age grave at Monkton Farleigh, Wilts. 1¾ in. diameter. Private collection (electrotype in Devizes Museum).

18 Gold disc from a Bell-Beaker grave at Mere, Wilts. 1½ in. diameter. Devizes Museum.

19 Early Bronze Age head-burial, with lower jaw detached and a flaked flint bar leaning against the skull, as reconstructed in Salisbury Museum, from Easton Down, Wilts.

20 Trepanned skull, with roundel removed from the skull, found in a Bell-beaker grave on Crichel Down, Dorset, photographed immediately after finding, 1938. Museum of the Royal College of Surgeons.

21 Four-footed pottery bowl found in a sand-pit together with the Bell-Beaker, no. 22, at Inkpen, Berks. Height 6¾ in. Newbury Museum.

22 Bell-beaker found with the four-footed bowl, no. 21, at Inkpen, Berks. Height 10¼ in. Newbury Museum.

23 Complete skeleton of dog, from the Early Bronze Age settlement-site on Easton Down, Wilts. Height at shoulder 15 in. Salisbury Museum.

24 Necked Beaker found with the food vessel no. 25 in a grave in Fargo Plantation, Wilts. Height 6 in. Salisbury Museum.

25 Food vessel found with the Necked Beaker no. 24 in the Fargo Plantation grave. Height 5 in. Salisbury Museum.

26 Oblique air view of Stonehenge from the south-west, showing the ditch and bank, the Aubrey Holes (white spots) and the central stone structures. The Heel Stone stands outside, by the road.

27 View looking southwards down the line of the West Kennet Avenue, Avebury, showing stones standing and re-erected, and sites of missing stones marked by concrete blocks.

28 The entrance stones of the Great Circle, Avebury, with the bank of the earthwork behind, looking south.

29 View of the stone structures of Stonehenge, looking south from the Outer Circle towards the bluestone Horseshoe and the Trilithons.

30 Dragging a replica bluestone on a sledge at Stonehenge, 1954.

31 Excavations on the line of the bluestone circle of Stonehenge, 1954, showing standing and fallen bluestones, and the stumps and sockets of others in the excavated area. The stone in the foreground is one of the two re-used bluestone lintels (no. 150).

32 Oblique air view of the Avebury circles from the north-west, showing the bank and ditch, the standing stones of the circles, and the modern village within the monument.

33 Carvings of a hafted dagger and two axe-blades (to right and bottom left) on Stone 53 of the sarsen trilithons at Stonehenge. The dagger is 12 in. in length.

34 Carvings of hafted daggers, flat axe-blades and cup-marks, on a sandstone slab from the Badbury Barrow, Dorset. The larger dagger is 12 in. in length. British Museum.

35 Underside of the bluestone lintel no. 36 at Stonehenge, showing mortise-holes visible during temporary excavation and lifting, 1954.

36 View in the inner area at Stonehenge, showing bluestone uprights of the Horseshoe setting, that on the left with a groove worked on its edge, and Trilithons in the background.

37 Oblique air view of a Disc Barrow completely excavated on Snail Down, Wilts., 1953. The regularly cut circular ditch is seen enclosing pits which held burials.

38 Wessex Culture cup of Manton type, with knobbed surface and perforations between the knobs, from a grave at Normanton, Wilts. 2¼ in. high. Devizes Museum.

39 Wessex Culture cup of Aldbourne type, with incised and punctuated ornament, from a grave on Oakley Down, Dorset. 1¾ in. high. Devizes Museum.

40 Wessex Culture cup with 'slashed' sides and cord-impressed decoration, from a grave at Normanton, Wilts. 1¾ in. high. Devizes Museum.

41 Equipment from a Wessex Culture warrior's grave, Bush Barrow, Normanton, Wilts., comprising two bronze dagger-blades, a bronze axe-head, and a mace or sceptre with polished stone head and shaft (reconstructed) inlaid with zigzag bone mounts. In the grave were also found the gold objects in Plate 42. Length of larger dagger, 14½ in. Devizes Museum.

42 Gold objects from the same burial as the objects in Plate 41, from Bush Barrow, Normanton, Wilts. The upper object is the gold plating of a belt-hook, and the large gold plate, 8½ in. across, lay on the man's chest, presumably sewn to a garment or corselet, and the smaller plate was probably similarly mounted. British Museum (electrotypes in Devizes Museum).

43 Head of mace or sceptre of polished jet or shale with inlaid gold studs, from a Wessex Culture grave in the Clandon Barrow, Dorset. Width 3 in. Also in the grave were other objects including an amber cup and the gold plate, Plate 44. Dorchester Museum.

44 Gold plate from the same Wessex Culture grave in the Clandon Barrow, Dorset, as the mace-head, Plate 43. The plate is 6 in. across, and like that from Bush Barrow (Plate 42) was probably sewn on a garment. Dorchester Museum.

45 Bronze axe-blade from a Wessex Culture burial in Barrow 7 on the Ridgeway, Dorset, with remains of finely woven woollen cloth on it, in which it had been wrapped. Length 3½ in. In the same grave were found bronze dagger-blades and the gold pommel-mount, Plate 46. Dorchester Museum.

46 Gold pommel-mount for a dagger, from a Wessex Culture burial in Barrow 7 on the Ridgeway, Dorset. Width 2 in. Found with bronze dagger-blades and the axe, Plate 45. Dorchester Museum.

47, 48 Bronze dagger-blade and knife-blade from a Wessex Culture burial at Winterbourne Stoke, Wilts. Length of dagger, 8½ in. Devizes Museum.

49, 50 Bronze dagger-blade and knife-blade from a Wessex Culture burial at Normanton, Wilts. Length of dagger, 8¾ in. Devizes Museum.

51 Amber cup from a Wessex Culture burial at Hove, Sussex. The cup is 3½ in. diameter, and was found in a hollowed tree-trunk coffin with a bronze dagger and stone battle-axe. Brighton Museum.

52 Gold cup from a Wessex Culture burial at Rillaton, Cornwall. The cup is 3½ in. high, and the handle fastened by rivets. British Museum.

53 Two cups of shale, from Wessex Culture burials probably in the Amesbury region of Wiltshire, 3½ and 3¾ in. high. Salisbury Museum.

54 Objects from a woman's grave of the Wessex Culture at Manton, Wilts. Above is a fragment of textile, and below three bronze awls; on the left a bronze knife-blade with a bone pommel, on the right, shale and stone beads. A string of shale disc-beads encircles a shale bead with gold inlaid bands, an amber disc in a gold mounting, and a pendant in the

form of a miniature halberd with gold-plated shaft and bronze blade. The knife-blade on the left is 1¼ in. long. Devizes Museum.

55 Amber beads and spacing-plates of a crescentic necklace from a Wessex Culture grave at Lake, Wilts. The largest spacing-plate is 3 in. across. British Museum.

56 Gold plate from a Wessex Culture burial at Upton Lovel, Wilts., 6 in. wide. British Museum (electrotype in Devizes Museum).

57 Objects from a woman's grave of the Wessex Culture at Normanton, Wilts. Above are pendants of amber, and centrally a large conical shale button with its gold casing (in two parts), and a gold object with criss-cross decoration. Below are two amber discs mounted in gold, as in the Manton burial (Plate 54), and a pendant in the form of a miniature halberd, made of amber with gold mounts, and a bronze blade, again similar to that from Manton. At the bottom is a gold-plated bronze pendant representing a miniature neck-ornament. The gold-mounted shale button is 1½ in. diameter. Devizes Museum.

58, 59 A cremated burial of the Wessex Culture at Stockbridge, Hants., as excavated. The upper photograph shows the inverted cinerary urn, and below, the cremated bones immediately on lifting the urn, with (in circle) a blue segmented faience bead. British Museum.

60 Reconstructed necklace from a Wessex Culture grave at Upton Lovel, Wilts., with beads of amber, shale and blue faience, of segmented and quoit forms. The quoit beads are ¾ in. across. Devizes Museum.

61 Middle Bronze Age cinerary urn from Bulford, Wilts. Height 13 in. Salisbury Museum.

62 Middle Bronze Age cinerary urn from Amesbury, Wilts. Height 12 in. Salisbury Museum.

63 Wessex Culture urn from Normanton, Wilts., found with an inhumation burial and ornaments of gold and amber. Height 8 in. Devizes Museum.

64, 65 Domestic vessels of the Late Bronze Age, from the settlement on Thorny Down, Wilts., $5\frac{1}{4}$ and $8\frac{3}{4}$ in. high. Salisbury Museum.

66 Late Bronze Age cinerary urn from a barrow near Stonehenge, $22\frac{3}{4}$ in. high. Devizes Museum.

67 Bronze twisted torc or neck-ornament, and bronze armlets of the Late Bronze Age, from Lake, Wilts. The torc is $5\frac{1}{4}$ in. diameter inside. Salisbury Museum.

68 Vertical view of a scale model of the excavated site of an Early Iron Age circular house and storage-pits at Little Woodbury, Wilts. The larger holes are pits for corn-storage (about 6 feet across), the smaller represent post-holes for the structure of a circular house some 40 feet across. Salisbury Museum.

69 Vertical air-photograph of the Early Iron Age hill-fort of Figsbury Rings, Wilts. The inner enclosure is a quarry-ditch used to heighten the main rampart in a secondary phase. The fort is 1050 ft. over-all.

70 Vertical air-photograph of the Early Iron Age hill-fort of Yarnbury Castle, Wilts. The main earthworks consist of multiple ramparts, some 1500 ft. over-all, with elaborate entrance outworks at the top right-hand corner, and a later enclosure at the bottom left. Inside the main defences can be seen faint traces of an earlier Iron Age earthwork, about 750 ft. across, and the grid pattern of the comparatively recent pens for the sheep fair held on the site.

71 Iron Age coinage (staters) of the tribe of the Durotriges. The top coin (two sides) is of gold, from the Chute hoard; the centre coin is silver, from Hanging Langford Camp, Wilts., the lower a bronze coin from Teffont Evias Quarry, Wilts. All $1\frac{1}{2}$ times actual size.

72 Oblique air view of the turf-cut figure known as the Giant of Cerne, Dorset. The outline of this figure of a club-bearing giant is cut down to the solid chalk, and is probably a representation of a native god in the period of the Roman Occupation. Above the giant can be seen a small earthwork enclosure, of unknown date.

Index